Endlings

Forerunners: Ideas First

Short books of thought-in-process scholarship, where intense analysis, questioning, and speculation take the lead

FROM THE UNIVERSITY OF MINNESOTA PRESS

Lydia Pyne
Endlings: Fables for the Anthropocene

Margret Grebowicz
Rescue Me: On Dogs and Their Humans

Sabina Vaught, Bryan McKinley Jones Brayboy, and Jeremiah Chin
The School–Prison Trust

After Oil Collective; Ayesha Vemuri and Darin Barney, Editors
Solarities: Seeking Energy Justice

Arnaud Gerspacher
The Owls Are Not What They Seem: Artist as Ethologist

Tyson E. Lewis and Peter B. Hyland
Studious Drift: Movements and Protocols for a Postdigital Education

Mick Smith and Jason Young
Does the Earth Care? Indifference, Providence, and Provisional Ecology

Caterina Albano
Out of Breath: Vulnerability of Air in Contemporary Art

Gregg Lambert
The World Is Gone: Philosophy in Light of the Pandemic

Grant Farred
Only a Black Athlete Can Save Us Now

Anna Watkins Fisher
Safety Orange

Heather Warren-Crow and Andrea Jonsson
Young-Girls in Echoland: #Theorizing Tiqqun

Joshua Schuster and Derek Woods
Calamity Theory: Three Critiques of Existential Risk

Daniel Bertrand Monk and Andrew Herscher
The Global Shelter Imaginary: IKEA Humanitarianism and Rightless Relief

Catherine Liu
Virtue Hoarders: The Case against the Professional Managerial Class

Christopher Schaberg
Grounded: Perpetual Flight . . . and Then the Pandemic

Marquis Bey
The Problem of the Negro as a Problem for Gender

Cristina Beltrán
**Cruelty as Citizenship: How Migrant Suffering
Sustains White Democracy**

Hil Malatino
Trans Care

Sarah Juliet Lauro
Kill the Overseer! The Gamification of Slave Resistance

Alexis L. Boylan, Anna Mae Duane, Michael Gill, and Barbara Gurr
Furious Feminisms: Alternate Routes on *Mad Max: Fury Road*

Ian G. R. Shaw and Marv Waterstone
Wageless Life: A Manifesto for a Future beyond Capitalism

Claudia Milian
LatinX

Aaron Jaffe
Spoiler Alert: A Critical Guide

Don Ihde
Medical Technics

Jonathan Beecher Field
Town Hall Meetings and the Death of Deliberation

Jennifer Gabrys
How to Do Things with Sensors

Naa Oyo A. Kwate
Burgers in Blackface: Anti-Black Restaurants Then and Now

Arne De Boever
Against Aesthetic Exceptionalism

Steve Mentz
Break Up the Anthropocene

John Protevi
Edges of the State

Claudia Milian
LatinX

(Continued on page 90)

Endlings
Fables for the Anthropocene

Lydia Pyne

University of Minnesota Press
MINNEAPOLIS
LONDON

ISBN 978-1-5179-1483-7 (PB)
ISBN 978-1-4529-6884-1 (Ebook)
ISBN 978-1-4529-6885-8 (Manifold)

Published by the University of Minnesota Press
111 Third Avenue South, Suite 290
Minneapolis, MN 55401–2520
www.upress.umn.edu

Available as a Manifold edition at manifold.umn.edu

The University of Minnesota is an equal-opportunity educator
and employer.

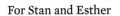
For Stan and Esther

Contents

Introduction: We Humans Are
a Storytelling Species   1

1. Species and Starts: Benjamin the
   Thylacine and Qi Qi the Baiji   11

2. Extinctions and Endings: Celia the Ibex
   and Lonesome George the Tortoise   31

3. Charisma and Character: Incas the Carolina
   Parakeet, Turgi the Tree Snail,
   and Wood's Cycad   53

Conclusion: How Do You Say
"Endling" in isiZulu?   73

Acknowledgments   81

Further Reading   83

Bibliography   85

Introduction: We Humans Are a Storytelling Species

IN THE BEGINNING WAS THE END.

Martha. Ben. Orange Band. 淇淇 (Qi Qi). Turgi. Incas and Lady Jane. Benjamin. George. Celia. Laña. Toughie. Lonesome George. Name after name after name.

These are names of the dead. Nicknames. Informal names. Certainly not names that the dead have given themselves. These are names that we humans have given—names we have bestowed, assigned, and conferred to the nonhuman animals whose stories we tell. Naming creates a familiarity between us and the dead.

These names are a way—fair or not—to lay claim to these animals and their stories; in a bit of dark, anthropocentric irony, perhaps we use these names to humanize them. And these particular names are a roll call of extinctions and endings on earth.

For billions of years, millions of species have come and gone as ecosystems have changed and evolutionary paths unfolded. We can see bits and pieces of these ancient species' stories through the fossil record. A bone here, an outline of an imprint there—an archive of life and death told through stones. Taken together, fossils show five mass-extinction events in earth's history; that is, five different events where large numbers of species died in a relatively short amount of time. The earliest was around 447 million years ago, during the late Ordovician; the most recent was at the end of the Cretaceous, roughly 66 million years ago, popularly known for bringing about the "end of the dinosaurs."

Fast-forward through deep time to today's Anthropocene, when humankind has inexorably altered the earth in ways that are unprecedented in the planet's 4.5-billion-year history. We are currently in the throes of what many scientists, journalists, thinkers, and concerned humans refer to as earth's sixth mass-extinction event. Unlike earlier extinctions, this one is driven by people—people and the havoc that their environmental and economic decisions have wreaked on the planet. The fossil record shows us the other five mass extinction events; the sixth we can watch in real time.[1]

Estimates vary of just how fast species are going extinct right now. At the beginning of the twenty-first century, the Millennium Ecosystem Assessment (a survey called for by the United Nations Secretary-General in 2000) estimated that twenty-four species a day went extinct. More recently, the United Nations Convention on Biological Diversity concluded that 150 species a day are lost.[2] Regardless of the precise number, it is safe to say that in the time it takes you to read this book, *at least* one species will have become extinct.

With so many extinctions, so much death, so much loss—what is so remarkable, then, about Martha, Benjamin, Lonesome George, and others like them? What makes these particular animal deaths so notable?

They are endlings—the last known individuals of their species.

Endling, itself, is a rather recent word.

In 1996, Robert M. Webster and Bruce Erickson wrote a letter to *Nature* proposing the word to fill a linguistic niche. "We need a

---

1. Kolbert, *The Sixth Extinction.*
2. "Global Extinction Rates: Why Do Estimates Vary So Wildly?," *Yale E360,* accessed September 13, 2021, https://e360.yale.edu/features/global _extinction_rates_why_do_estimates_vary_so_wildly.

word to designate the last person, animal, or other species in his/her/its lineage," they wrote. "We do not have one word to describe the last person surviving or deceased in a family line, or the last survivor of a species."[3]

At the time, Webster and Erickson were working at the Christian City Convalescent Center in Union City, Georgia, where a patient, reflecting on his own imminent mortality, remarked, "I am the last of my line."[4] (Trying to come up with a word apropos of himself and his situation, the patient proposed that he might be an "omega," but Webster and Erickson worried that "omega" was not a word sufficiently unique to capture the last-ness of what the person was experiencing.) Webster and Erikson informally polled their colleagues and others in medically adjacent fields for word possibilities and compiled a short list that included: *lastoline* (a contraction for "last of the line"); *yatim* (Arabic for "orphan" or "unique of its kind"); *ender* ("one who ends or finishes"); or even *endler*.

Ultimately, *endling* was the word that stuck. It just fit. *Endling* was the right portmanteau of *end-* and *-ling*. *End* is self-explanatory. The *-ling* suffix means, in a general sense, "a person or thing belonging to or to be concerned about" when attached to a prefix noun. In Old and Middle English, for example, the word *æðeling* (atheling) combined *æðel-* (family) and *-ing* to refer to a person who belonged to a noble family or an heir apparent to the throne. A more recent instance, *foundling,* combines *found-* and *-ling* where the *Oxford English Dictionary* defines a foundling as "a deserted infant whose parents are unknown, a child whom there is no one to claim."[5]

The word *endling* is "Tolkienesque," science journalist Michelle Nijhuis summarized in *The New Yorker* in 2017, "like Halfling or Enting, evoking a lost world."[6] This otherworld-ness of the word is

---

3. Webster and Erickson, "The Last Word?" 386.

4. Webster and Erickson.

5. "Foundling, n." and "Atheling, n.," in *OED Online*, accessed September 13, 2021, http://www.oed.com/.

6. Nijhuis, "What Do You Call the Last of a Species?"

no doubt part of its appeal. It's familiar and new at the same time. It's cure and it sounds diminutive, almost like a term of endearment—the sound of the word elicits an emotional response, perhaps wanting to be protective of the organism in question. "The sound of endling as a word would turn out to be a large part of its attraction," environmental historian Dolly Jørgensen notes.[7]

Endling is a word that sticks with people the first time they hear it or say it out loud. When I introduce people to the word ("I'm writing a book about endlings"), I catch myself pronouncing it slowly and carefully, emphasizing the *l* to make sure the listener is not confusing *endling* with *ending*. People would repeat "endling" back haltingly, out loud, pronouncing it with the careful precision of learning a word in a new language. It took months for Microsoft Word and my phone to stop autocorrecting "endling" into something else.

For years after its invention, however, the word languished.[8] Although its usage and popularity have grown over the last two decades, the *Oxford English Dictionary* and other formal, gatekeeping institutions of language have yet to include the word in their catalogs. (Even a contemporary search of the *OED* in 2021 still results in "No dictionary entries found for 'endling.'") At the beginning of the twenty-first century, *endling* was simply a word without cultural narrative—like a character without its own story.

This changed in 2001 with a gallery exhibit at the National Museum of Australia called Tangled Destinies that introduced museum-goers to the interplay between environment, technology, and social history of Australia and Tasmania. The gallery was designed by Mike Smith, an archaeologist and senior curator who joined the National Museum of Australia in 1996. The exhibit highlighted the extinction of the thylacine species—*Thylacinus cynocephalus* or the Tasmanian tiger—that was hunted to extinction by nineteenth- and early twentieth-century British settlers

7. Jørgensen, "Endling, the Power of the Last in an Extinction-Prone World."

8. Nijhuis, "What Do You Call the Last of a Species?"

in Tasmania. At the center of the exhibit was Benjamin, the last known thylacine, who died in captivity in 1936 at Beaumaris Zoo in Hobart. In the exhibit, Benjamin was labeled as an "endling" and presented as the final chapter—the conclusion, if you will—to the story of the thylacines' extinction. It was here that endlings found their extinction narrative, and extinction narratives had found new protagonists.

The word and its cachet have long outgrown the original letter in *Nature*. Today, the "endling" is used almost exclusively in reference to nonhuman organisms—animals, and occasionally plants, that have been identified as the last vestige of their species. "The endling label puts extinction on the human scale—it gives an animal a name, recognizes its worth, and asks for the human to empathize with the imminent end of a whole animal's line," Jørgensen offers. "The word recognizes the permanence of group extinction on an individual level."[9]

"The last pure dusky seaside sparrow died today, ending a steady drift toward extinction of the little bird that refused to yield to man's intrusion," *The New York Times* published on June 17, 1987. "Orange Band, named for the colored band used to tell him from the other four [males], was the last."[10] Before endling was even the word to describe Orange Band, the *Times* marked the extinction of *Ammodramus maritimus nigrescens* with the death of its last surviving member in a short "obituary" for the species at the bottom of page A20 in the *Times*, below an article about tax evasion and to the left of a report of a gubernatorial divorce. For Orange Band, the story of the birds' extinction was—and is today—told as one of habitat loss. The birds only lived in a limited, ten-mile stretch of Florida's eastern coastal marshes that had been overtaken by the

9. Jørgensen, "Endling, the Power of the Last in an Extinction-Prone World."

10. "Last of the Dusky Sparrows Dies," accessed April 13, 2021, http://timesmachine.nytimes.com/timesmachine/1987/06/17/974787.html.

space program at nearby Cape Canaveral; people were unaccom-modating to the birds, and the birds were unable to survive outside of their narrow range.

Orange Band was hardly the only one. Martha the passenger pigeon, *Ectopistes migratorius,* named after the original First Lady of the United States, Martha Washington, died on September 1, 1914. "Booming Ben," a heath hen, *Tympanuchus cupido cupido,* was last seen on March 11, 1932 in Martha's Vineyard, Massachusetts. Celia the Pyrenean ibex, *Capra pyrenaica pyrenaica,* died in the Spanish Pyrenees on January 6, 2000. In 1996, the *Chicago Tribune* reported that Turgi, the last *Partula turgida,* a Polynesian tree snail species, died. ("It moved at a rate of less than 2 feet a year so it took a while for the curators at London Zoo to be sure it had stopped moving forever . . . The Polynesian tree snail is extinct after the last sur-vivor of the species passed away in a plastic box at the zoo . . . [it] will have a tombstone inscribed '1.5 million years BC to January 1996' to mark its passing."[11]) 淇淇 (Qi Qi) the baiji—the Yangtze river dolphin or *Lipotes vexillifer*—died in 2002 at the Institute of Hydrobiology in Wuhan, China. Sudan, the last male northern white rhino, *Ceratotherium simum cottoni,* was euthanized by veter-inarians at the Ol Pejeta Conservancy in Kenya on Monday, March 19, 2018. George, the last known *Achatinella apexfulva,* a species of O'ahu tree snail, died on January 1, 2019.

Because the end of every endling story is the same, it's easy to assume that the stories that get to that end must be the same as well. It's comfortable for us to read endling stories as an inevitable arc of death, varying only in the details, like whether it's a story of an ibex or a treefrog. In the end, this simplistic narrative goes, endlings die as a result of human action or, perhaps more damning, inaction. "Endlings are avatars of loss," science journalist Ed Yong notes.[12]

11. "Tiny Tree Snail Finally Creeps to Extinction," accessed May 14, 2021, https://www.chicagotribune.com/news/ct-xpm-1996-02-01 -9602020105-story.html.
    12. Yong, "The Last of Its Kind."

Why do stories about endlings matter?

"Storytelling is a human universal," a team of anthropologists conclude in a 2017 study published in *Nature*. "The universal presence and antiquity of storytelling indicates that it may be an important human adaptation."[13] In other words, we humans are a storytelling species. "There are countless forms of narrative in the world," French philosopher and literary theorist Roland Barthes notes. ". . . indeed narrative starts with the very history of mankind; there is not, there has never been anywhere, any people without narrative; all classes, all human groups, have their stories, and very often those stories are enjoyed by men of different and even opposite cultural backgrounds."[14]

But what, then, is a story? How do we tell it? How do we hear it? Why do certain "types" of stories—or literary devices—work particularly well?

On a fundamental level, narratives are built out of parts—story elements like an arc or plot, the development of characters, building tension and conflict, and, of course, resolution or catharsis. Although philosophers have debated the nature of storytelling since Aristotle, the twentieth century saw a burst of research from literary theorists like Vladimir Propp, Claude Lévi-Strauss, Joseph Campbell, and Tzvetan Todorov (to name a few) who proposed ways to think about the most essential elements of narratives—the building blocks of stories—particularly stories like myths (*mythos*), fairy tales, and folk stories.

Many of these theorists argued, there are particular ways that the building blocks of those narratives are assembled over the centuries that become familiar and even predictable. (For example, a heroic journey, a trickster sowing discord, a magical intervention, a lesson learned.) Perhaps, then, in the case of endlings, as we try to work

13. Smith et al., "Cooperation and the Evolution of Hunter-Gatherer Storytelling," 1853.

14. Barthes and Duisit, "An Introduction to the Structural Analysis of Narrative," 237.

out how to treat them as characters and how to tell their stories, we borrow what is familiar and predictable. As Barthes points out, "Narration can indeed receive its meaning only from the world which makes use of it."[15]

As a storytelling species, we tell stories about ourselves, our environments, the animals in our environments, the things we encounter, the things we feel, and the things we imagine. Some stories offer cosmologies, morals, and lessons—others offer satire and entertainment. Over the evolution of our species, humankind has told its stories using a plethora of tropes that have evolved with us. Narrative, according to Barthes, might be universal, but the specifics of stories can vary considerably across time, space, and culture.

Endlings, as we've come to shape them, are creatures steeped in pathos, gravitas, and tragedy. But endlings are more complicated characters than simple tragic heroes and are more varied in narrative than we might assume at first glance. Each individual endling—Benjamin, Turgi, Orange Band, and the like—is unique in its biography and singular in the twists and turns of its species's evolutionary history. Unpack the story of an endling and you will find more stories—their species, evolutionary history, cultural cachet, beginnings, and endings—nestled inside each other like matryoshka dolls.

In the decades since the word was first proposed in *Nature,* "endling" has grown to become a powerful, emotional character in contemporary Anthropocene storytelling. "The concept of endling as the last of a species holds cultural power," Dolly Jørgensen notes, "encouraging its mobilization in a world facing extinction around every corner."[16] Today organisms are named—witnessed—in order to be remembered and not be forgotten.

15. Barthes and Duisit, 264.
16. Jørgensen, "Endling, the Power of the Last in an Extinction-Prone World."

When Lonesome George, the last Pinta Island Galápagos tortoise died in 2012, for example, media reports invariably decried the extinction of the species and the anthropogenic reasons for it. The stories would eulogize Lonesome George and remind readers about the fragility of Galápagos ecosystems—the other tortoises and species currently under threat of extinction. In such tellings, Lonesome George is a warning that, if we're not careful, other Galápagos species will dwindle down to their own endlings. (Incidentally, Wikipedia notes that Lonesome George is best known for "being an endling.")

"In the context of extinction, these kinds of stories are not an attempt to obscure the truth of the situation, but to insist on a truth that is not reducible to populations and data," philosopher Thom Van Dooren describes of his approach to writing about extinction, which he says was heavily influenced by practices of literary witnessing that surround Shoah (Holocaust) and genocide writing. "In place of an approach that aims for an impartial or 'objective' recitation of the 'facts' . . . our stories [can] play a role of witness or testimony to the suffering and death of others." This sort of witnessing is a form of truth-telling about extinction and loss; one that Van Dooren argues "might draw us all into a greater sense of accountability."[17]

But this begs the question of what endling stories we tell, who tells them, and how they're told. As we tell endling stories, we are inevitably drawing from established, familiar literary tropes. What endlings offer us now is the potential for careful, deliberate storytelling about extinction in the Anthropocene. As we tell stories about endlings, we should ask ourselves: Do we want endlings to be agents of change? Tragic heroes? The animals that hold up the cosmos? Virgil-like guides for taking us through the circle of hell that is the sixth mass extinction? Aesop's fables for the Anthropocene?

17. Van Dooren, *Flight Ways,* 9–10.

Or is there a yet-to-be-told story that is unique and specific to the organism that is the last of its kind?

Over the past two decades, *endling* has moved out of its initial museum discourse. Artists, musicians, poets, and a plethora of others have found the word and the idea of a "last of its kind" has prompted a very human response, be it music, art, poetry, or the like.[18] With these encounters, we continue to shape, write, and frame endling encounters here in the Anthropocene.

Ultimately, endling stories are the stories of species and how they end. These stories also mirror how we tell stories about extinction; they are ways that humankind marks loss, harm, and environmental trauma that our own species has inflicted on other species. But endlings are also individual organisms with their own evolutionary and cultural histories. They are Ben, Martha, Celia, Toughie, and the dozens and dozens of individuals that die every day without names but are, nevertheless, the last of their species.

These are their stories so far. And the stories of their stories.

18. Jørgensen, "Endling, the Power of the Last in an Extinction-Prone World."

1. Species and Starts: Benjamin the Thylacine and Qi Qi the Baiji

DEAD. DEAD. ALMOST DEAD. A species on life support. Extinct. Inevitably going extinct. More dead. Still dead. Just . . . dead.

This is how we tend to frame stories about endlings. The last individual dies, the species becomes extinct; it's a tragedy, the story goes, a tragedy caused by people doing irreparable harm to nonhumans.

It's easy to assume that is how stories about endlings have to be told—in no small way because that's how they have always been told, even before *endling* was a word. In fact, the very nature of what makes an endling an endling encourages this sort of storytelling, framing endlings around death and extinction. But this sort of story can do endlings a disservice by treating the endling organisms as interchangeable characters whose entire purpose is to die in order to move the story along. This is unimaginative storytelling. It doesn't offer endlings the narrative intricacy that such a complex organism requires.

Endlings are stories within stories within stories—they are a multitude of beginnings, endings, and everything in between. They are more than just "dead" organisms and tragic tales.

Endlings—as we've come to identify them, write about them, and talk about them—begin with Benjamin, the last thylacine.

In historical records, thylacines are often called Tasmanian wolves, tigers, or hyenas due to their dark, distinctive stripes running from behind the shoulders to the tail. Thylacines had short, rounded ears, powerful jaws, and dense, short fur. As marsupials—like kangaroos, koalas, and wombats—female thylacines carried their joeys in a back-opening pouch. Hunting mainly at night, thylacines pursued prey like other marsupials, small rodents, and birds that lived at the edges of their woodland habitats. Life expectancy of a noncaptive thylacine was something like five to seven years.

Although "endlings" might have originated with Benjamin, Benjamin's story actually starts much earlier than the 2001 Tangled Destinies exhibit in the National Museum of Australia. Earlier than his death in 1936 at the Beaumaris Zoo in Tasmania. Much earlier than the decades of debate about whether or not his species is really, truly, completely, and absolutely extinct. (Unconfirmed sightings of thylacines persist even today.) The story of Benjamin is older, even, than the arrival of European settlers in what is now called Australia and Tasmania in the eighteenth, nineteenth, and twentieth centuries.

The real origin of Benjamin's story is roughly eighteen million years ago, during the Miocene, when several thylacine species were found across Australia, Tasmania, and as far north as what is now Papua New Guinea. Fast-forward millions of years and several thylacine species could still be found on the mainland of Australia, until a little over three thousand years ago, when those species became extinct. Researchers cite multiple pressures for the extinction of thylacines on mainland Australia—pressures like changes in human land use, fire regime, and hunting practices, competition pressure from the dingo, and an abrupt shift in climate due to the El Niño Southern Oscillation.[1]

Thylacines appear in ancient Aboriginal rock art at several locations in Australia. Some of the petroglyphs—estimated to be

---

1. Douglass S. Rovinsky, email interview with author, February 9, 2022.

thousands of years old—show thylacines nursing joeys and feeding their young. One petroglyph from Australia's Northern Territory even depicts a thylacine with a three-pronged hunting spear in its back.[2] Some archaeologists suggest that thylacines in rock art—especially at the red rock of Murujuga, the largest archaeological site in the world—were a way that Aboriginal peoples documented an extinction even as they were witnessing it, as thylacine populations died out across Australia thousands of years ago.[3]

Oral histories from the Adnyamathanha peoples in the Flinders Range of South Australia suggest that thylacines could even have survived in the area into the 1830s.[4] "Today *marrukurli* [thylacines] are known only as mammals of the Dreaming. That is, there is no one living who claims to have seen one," linguist Dorothy Tunbridge noted in her work with the Nepabunna Aboriginal School, documenting the names of Flinders Range animals in the Adnyamathanha language. "Both the Dreaming and other oral tradition, however, suggest the possibility of their bodily existence in the region in the not-too-distant past."[5]

Benjamin's species—*Thylacinus cynocephalus*—was present across Sahul (the landmass that includes New Guinea, mainland Australia, and Tasmania) from around 2 million years ago and survived several thousand years longer in Tasmania than it did on mainland Australia. When Tasmania became isolated from Australia with the appearance of the Bass Strait, roughly twelve thousand years ago, the island's geographic isolation became a refugia for a plethora of species like the thylacine. (Thus ensuring that such species survived at least into the nineteenth century.)[6] Historical estimates suggest that there was a population of roughly five thou-

2. Paddle, *The Last Tasmanian Tiger,* 18–19.
3. González Zarandona, *Murujuga,* 53.
4. Paddle, *The Last Tasmanian Tiger,* 23.
5. Paddle, 23.
6. "National Museum of Australia—Separation of Tasmania," accessed May 17, 2021, https://www.nma.gov.au/defining-moments/resources/separation-of-tasmania.

sand thylacine individuals when European explorers arrived on
Tasmania—what is called Iutruwita in Palawa kani, a contemporary
reconstructed Tasmanian language—before those languages and
their peoples were exterminated.[7]

Most of what we know about thylacine behavior comes from
colonial-era records from what was then the British colony of Van
Diemen's Land. (The colony was renamed "Tasmania" in 1856 with
the cessation of transported convict labor the year before.) Some of
these thylacine observations were accurate, some not; many were
embellished and exaggerated by the time they reached scientific
circles back in Europe. Early nineteenth-century naturalists working on the island were prickly about the misinformation about the
area's flora and fauna they saw in print. The famous nineteenth-
century French naturalist Georges Cuvier, for example, described
the thylacine as a marine predator, despite scant field evidence for
the claim.[8]

Unfortunately, there are no nineteenth-century records written by Aboriginal Tasmanian peoples, or then-contemporary interviews, about their thoughts regarding thylacines. The primary
source of written records that describe interactions between
Aboriginal Tasmanian peoples and thylacines was created by an
English amateur anthropologist George Augustus Robinson in the
1830s. (It is important to note that any discussion of Robinson's
historical legacy needs to consider his actions in 1832 that forced
what remained of the island's Aboriginal Tasmanian peoples to re-
locate to the nearby Flinders Island. The devastation of Aboriginal
populations between 1832 and 1838 has been described by historians as genocide.[9]) Robinson's records showed that different
Aboriginal communities interacted with and viewed the thylacine

7. "Extinction of Thylacine | National Museum of Australia," accessed
September 13, 2021, https://www.nma.gov.au/defining-moments/resources
/extinction-of-thylacine.
8. Paddle, *The Last Tasmanian Tiger,* 26–29.
9. Lawson, *The Last Man,* 20.

in a plethora of ways. However, none of the recorded Aboriginal Tasmanians' encounters with thylacines showed the animals to be reviled and hunted the way they would come to be with European settlers.[10]

By the mid-nineteenth century, thylacines were quickly becoming animals—objects, really—of dread among the British colonists and were viciously exterminated as such. Thylacines were viewed with suspicion and terror, living in settler lore as blood-sucking vampires or a fearsome werewolf-like creatures. (There are occasional references to thylacine blood-feeding in scientific literature that persisted into the mid-twentieth century; but, by and large, "vampire thylacines" were something that existed only in the minds of European settlers.) To those settlers, thylacines were a malevolent and almost mythical creatures.[11]

The colonial government formally issued a bounty for thylacines in 1888—one pound for adult thylacines and ten shillings for juveniles. In order to collect the bounty, a person had to produce the skin of the thylacine with the head, scalp, and paws still attached; once the skinned thylacine was validated by a colonial official, a hole was punched in the arm of the skin.[12] (Ostensibly, this would ensure that no one could claim a bounty on the same thylacine skin more than once.) In the 1880s, the skin of one adult thylacine would be worth three days' wage for a skilled tradesperson. (In 2017, this was worth approximately £66.18 as 3 days' wage for a skilled tradesperson would be, roughly, $100.) Contemporary historians and scientists note that the thylacines did not, in fact, pose as much a threat to setters' sheep—a popular reason given for eradicating the thylacines—as settlers might have liked to think they did.

10. Paddle, *The Last Tasmanian Tiger*, 32.

11. Paddle, 32.

12. "The Thylacine Museum—History: Persecution (Page 6)," accessed September 14, 2021, http://www.naturalworlds.org/thylacine /history/persecution/persecution_6.htm; "National Museum of Australia— Extinction of Thylacine," accessed May 17, 2021, https://www.nma.gov.au /defining-moments/resources/extinction-of-thylacine.

Although the bounty scheme was officially disbanded in 1909—spurred by concerns about the rarity of the animal, its potential extinction, and a growing horror at the slaughter of Tasmanian animals—the damage to the species was irreversible. Between the introduction of species that competed with thylacines (like wild dogs), diseases like mange (disease wiped out sixteen of the seventeen thylacines at the Melbourne Zoo by 1903), and extensive habitat destruction due to settlers' unsustainable farming and sheep-raising, to say nothing of the thousands of thylacines killed outright by humans (historical estimates suggest that settlers killed around 3,500 individuals), the species inevitably went extinct in the first half of the twentieth century.

The treatment of the thylacine—the story of the species and the first steps toward its extinction, the beginning of its end—is colonial violence in a microcosm.

And this brings us to Benjamin. By 1934, the Beaumaris Zoo in Hobart had the last captive thylacine of the last thylacine species in the world. Two years later, thylacines would be considered extinct.

The first record of a thylacine on public display appears in the *Hobart Town Courier* on the September 17, 1831. ("A beautiful specimen of the male TIGER of Van Diemen's Land, is now to be seen at George Marsden's Livery Stables [opposite to Mr. Swan's] Elizabeth Street. No live Tiger has ever been exhibited or seen in Hobart town before."[13]) By 1850, a plethora of thylacines had been exported to zoos—and zoological gardens—throughout mainland Australia, Europe, the United Kingdom, North America, and India. Historical estimates suggest that something like 224 individual thylacines could be found at fourteen international zoos, although finding specific records make it difficult to pin down an exact number.

13. "Classified Advertising," *Hobart Town Courier*, September 17, 1831, http://nla.gov.au/nla.news-article4202126.

In the 1920s, many of the animals on display at the Beaumaris Zoo came from the private animal collection of Mrs. Mary Grant Roberts, who championed the welfare of Tasmania's fauna, particularly its birds and thylacines. (When Mrs. Roberts spoke to the *Hobart Daily Post* on October 30, 1909, she described "the rare and handsome Tasmanian tigers" as a "species now almost extinct."[14]) After her death in November 1921, her menagerie was presented to Hobart City Council—with the agreement that the Tasmanian government would offer a subsidy toward its upkeep. The city council relocated the zoo to the Queens Domain in the city and hired Arthur Reid to be the animals' curator. Reid was assisted for years, unofficially, by his daughter Alison.[15]

By 1931, the zoo had only one remaining thylacine on exhibit. That same year, the Hobart City Council Reserves Committee (the committee that oversaw procurement and logistics of the zoo's animals, among other city businesses) was able to procure a second thylacine—this second animal would come to be known as Benjamin. Minutes from the committee are not preserved between 1932 and 1934, so details about the animal's provenance, age, and sex have been lost. Upon the thylacine's arrival at Beaumaris, Australian naturalist David Fleay took some photographs and filmed the animal for about sixty-two seconds; Fleay promptly received a bite on his own, human hindquarters for his troubles.

When Arthur Reid died in December 1935, the misogynistic Hobart City Council Reserves Committee, under the direction of Bruce Lipcombe, refused to employ a woman as curator, despite the fact that Reid's daughter, Alison, was more than qualified. Her expertise was indispensable to the zoo and the health of the animals. The Reserves Committee allowed Alison and her mother to

14. Paddle, *The Last Tasmanian Tiger*, 169.

15. Eric Guiler, "Cultural Advice," in *Australian Dictionary of Biography*, accessed May 22, 2021, https://adb.anu.edu.au/biography /roberts-mary-grant-8228.

live in the curator's cottage on the zoo's grounds rent-free, as long as Alison was willing to continue to work—unpaid.[16]

Alison took their offer. The effectiveness of her work, however, was severely curtailed when the committee appropriated her keys to the animals' enclosures and only allowed her to work during the zoo's "normal business hours." (This was problematic, as animals' care and welfare could not necessarily be neatly slotted into the seven hours the zoo was open. Some animals, for example, were nocturnal.) When the Reids' financial situation became truly grim, the council begrudgingly offered a small gratuity as payment to them for an assault that Arthur Reid had suffered years prior thwarting poachers at the zoo.

Over the next year and a half, decisions the Reserves Committee made were disastrous to the animals at the zoo, despite Alison Reid's heroic, ceaseless attempts to advocate for the animals. Cages went uncleaned. Animals were underfed or left to eat the previous day's rotten food before being fed again. Veterinary treatments were denied, citing cost. Employees were unmotivated and careless. Animals died. Whether the committee's decisions were made from indifference, apathy, or hollow-ringing attempts of frugality, the effects were the same. Alison protested, wrote letters, demanded keys, and, ultimately, was fired from her unpaid job.

By winter 1936, the situation was dire for both Alison and the zoo's animals. Dismissed and turned out of her home in the midst of the raging Great Depression, Alison was completely powerless to do anything more listen to the nightly distress calls of the zoo's carnivores. The thylacine, a Bengal tiger, and a pair of lions were frequently shut outside, left in the open to face the cold, rain, and snow of Hobart's particularly severe winter without covering, protection, or access to their dens. Those in charge—specifically, the men in charge—simply could not be bothered. In interviews recorded decades later, Alison's voice still choked with emotion, describing the cruelty and neglect of the animals' conditions.

16. Paddle, *The Last Tasmanian Tiger,* 189.

Finally, on September 7, 1936, in the freezing night air and locked out of its den, the world's last known thylacine died. Fifty-nine days earlier, the government of Tasmania extended an official protected status to the species, but it was too little, too late. Incidentally, the zoo went defunct in 1937.[17]

Bruce Lipscombe reported to the Reserves Committee the following week that "the body [of the thylacine] had been forwarded to the Museum," per the committee's minutes.[18] But it appears that the Museum was uninterested in Benjamin and made no effort to reserve any part of it, so confident were they that other thylacines remains could be obtained. (The skin that appeared in the 2001 Tangled Destinies exhibit, called the Old New Land exhibit until it closed in 2020, was from a different thylacine individual.) The material remains of Benjamin, like his species writ large, are gone.

On February 10, 1937, the Fauna Board—a conservation and wildlife organization, under the direction of naturalists J. E. C. Lord, Joseph Pearson, and A. K. Butler—made the decision to publicize the extinction of the thylacine in the hopes that it might generate some reliable sighting or information about the continued existence of the species. The subsequent radio and newspaper campaign yielded nothing that could be substantiated; indeed decades of rumors and attempts to find thylacines have been futile for almost ninety years.

The thylacine species, *Thylacinus cynocephalus,* was eventually declared extinct by the International Union for the Conservation of Nature in 1982 and by the Tasmanian government four years later in 1986. "The absence of presence was officially declared as the presence of absence," environmental historian Dolly Jørgensen summarized the thylacine extinction. "While there has been official agreement on the end of the thylacine, sighting reports continue to this day."[19]

17. "Extinction of Thylacine | National Museum of Australia.".

18. Paddle, *The Last Tasmanian Tiger,* 196.

19. Jørgensen, "Presence of Absence, Absence of Presence, and Extinction Narratives," 53–54

Although we talk about the thylacine endling today as "Benjamin," that part of the story comes decades after the animal's death. Curiously—almost unbelievably—"Benjamin" was born via a radio interview in 1968 when Frank Darby, a Victoria resident with no apparent ties to zoos or wildlife conservation, gave an interview with famed Australian naturalist Graham Pizzey. In the interview, Darby asserted that he had been the keeper of the last thylacine at the zoo in Hobart and claimed that the zoo had used "Benjamin"— "Benjy"—as a pet name for the thylacine. "He said he used to feed Benjy a live rabbit night and morning," a May 1968 newspaper article quoted Darby as saying. "He was tame, could be patted, but was morose, and showed no affection."[20]

Every single detail Darby offered about the zoo and the thylacine were wrong. Demonstrably, completely, and utterly wrong. The thylacine was female (per interviews and a careful examination of historical photographs, although recent analysis of Fleay's film footage has raised more questions about the thylacine's sex than it answers), the zoo was not in the business of offering its carnivores live prey (this would have been a huge ethical breach, even in the 1930s), and the enclosure was a different layout from his description (it was smaller than what Darby described).[21] For decades, Alison Reid and others have consistently pointed out that the plethora of falsehoods in Frank Darby's thylacine claims, including that no one, ever, had called the thylacine "Benjamin."

It's astonishing to consider how much and how little we know about Benjamin. We know "he" was an endling. That his species extinction was the result of colonial cruelty and environmental carelessness. That "he" is now called "Benjamin" and "Benjamin" quickly became an icon for environmental conservation in Australia. And, in recent decades, we know "Benjamin" was the endling that

20. Paddle, *The Last Tasmanian Tiger,* 198.
21. Sleightholme, "Confirmation of the Gender of the Last Captive Thylacine," 953–56; Paddle, *The Last Tasmanian Tiger.*

made people sit up and take stock of what the word *endling* afforded
the us in terms of Anthropocene storytelling.

And yet the mythos of Benjamin endures and grows—at this point,
perhaps more myth than history, more story than science. What is
undeniably true, however, is that "Benjamin" is a set of interlinked
and nested stories that, like all good stories, offers its audiences a
way to think about extinction and loss of species in nuanced ways.

Species are a human construct.

At its most basic, a species is a category. It's a way of grouping
similar populations of individuals together. Over the past few millennia, we've continuously divvied and re-divvied living things into
categories of individuals that are "most alike" in order to describe
different populations of organisms on earth; naming and categoriz-
ing species is called taxonomy. According to historians and philosophers of biology, Western intellectual traditions have been working
with the idea of "species" since Plato and Aristotle. (Plato's student
Theophrastus [ca. 372–287 BCE], for example, created the first systematic attempt to classify the botanical world, classifying plants
based on shape of plant parts as well as by their practical, everyday
uses.) If we're going to define endlings as the last individuals of a
species, it's worth unpacking what a species is.

The modern—and even medieval—word for "species" is a Latin
translation of the Greek word *eidos*; this has, in turn, translates into
"idea," "kind," "sort," or "form."[22] It's crucial to note that thinking
about and creating categories in the natural world isn't solely the
purview of modern, Western science. How we talk about species—
indeed the history of "species concepts"—tilts heavily toward traditional Western sources, despite a plethora of work in non-Western
cultures to systematically classify organisms.

Historically, "species" draws from Plato's definition of Form
(again, *eidos*) that emphasizes how a form is unchanging and

22. Wilkins, *Defining Species,* and Wilkins, *Species.*

separated from similar forms. Perhaps more than anything else, Plato's system of classifying forms by following a binary system of contraries—what we might, today, call a decision tree—informs how we think about species on earth. With enough questions, and enough characteristics, we can find what separates one form from another.

Over the ensuing centuries, natural philosophers—like Pliny the Elder, Porphyry, and Boëthius—pushed this concept further into the types and things that a form could entail, specifically using the term *genos* ("genus" today) as a broader category for classification than *eidos* or species. Interestingly, within this classifying logic, species do not begin because their form is a universal constant thing. By the Middles Ages, "species" populated medieval bestiaries, which were often moral homilies as well as herbal pharmacopeia that carefully noted plants that could be used for medicinal or culinary reasons. In those instances, describing "species" wasn't simply an act of classifying organisms for the sake of classifying organisms; they documented how people interacted with and used nonhuman species like plants.

Additionally, folk taxonomies, for example, have long offered important, legitimate ways of describing "species" that might not easily slot into how a species has been defined historically; they depend on everyday, social knowledge.[23] "The folk taxonomy of the Tzeltal Maya of Mexico, for example, labels both local conifer species 'pine,' yet identified five different subspecific varieties of their most important food plant: corn (*Zea mays*)," botanist Nanci Ross offers by way of an example. "Classifying is integral to our understanding of our world."[24]

Historically, how we think about species can be roughly divided into two major parts: prebiology and postbiology. Specifically, seventeenth-century English naturalist John Ray claimed species

23. Phaka et al., "Folk Taxonomy and Indigenous Names for Frogs in Zululand, South Africa," 17.

24. Ross, "'What's That Called?,'" 123.

ought to be classified based on similarities and differences rather than preconceived notions of forms. By the time Swedish naturalist Carl Linnaeus (Carl von Linné) formalized binomial nomenclature in 1735—the genus-species system we use today for naming organisms—"species" were things to be found, described, and categorized in the natural world. Fast-forward to Darwin and evolutionary theory (and what we might see as "biology") and species could be understood as things in process. And if species were a process, they could begin and end.

Like any category, though, what makes a species a species is ultimately a set—sets—of human decisions made and remade over time. In contemporary scientific literature, there are twenty-six formal—and different!—definitions for what a "species" is.[25] (Some species concepts emphasize the historical, evolutionary element of a lineage; some emphasize the affinities of genes between organisms; nondimensional species concepts, like folk taxonomies, emphasize different everyday interactions and knowledges, depending on cultural contexts.[26]) For practical purposes, species are pragmatic and necessary for the business of doing science as well as conservation legislation. Species allow scientists to analyze how populations of organisms change over time, to note new organisms (newly discovered species), and, of course, mark their extinction.

But—and this is key to thinking about endlings—species are also narrative. Species have a beginning, a middle, and an end—in effect, an origin, a life history, and an extinction. (For many extinct species, they also have an afterlife; they are memorialized, commemorated, celebrated, or even mourned.) The narrative of a species offers endlings their very outermost layer of story. We couldn't have species without endlings or endlings without species. It's how and why Benjamin's story actually starts some 18 million years before the Beaumaris Zoo.

25. Wilkins, *Defining Species*, 193.
26. Wilkins, 194–97.

Although species have all of these narrative elements—a beginning, a middle, and an end—those points are notoriously difficult to
pin down both biologically and literarily. It turns out, for example,
that even an endling needs an origin story. So what would that beginning look like? When does a species begin? When does it end?
What sorts of origin stories and conclusions will we find? Which
will be cast as tragic heroes in the face of the sixth mass extinction?
How much does one inform the other?

We might have invented a word to mark the end of a species but
finding the origin of one is an altogether different question. There
isn't a *begin-ling* or equivalent word to frame how we think and
write about species' biological beginning; what's more, it turns out
that finding the literal origin of a specific species is impossible.
(Contemporary philosopher Timothy Morton offers, "so dire is
the paradox of evolution that Darwin should have used some kind
of wink emoticon, had one been available, and scare quote: The
'Origin' of 'Species'.) The punchline of Darwin's book is that there
are no species and they have no origin."[27] Morton's point is about
the arbitrariness of human-created categories and how difficult
those categories—origins, species—are to define when you get right
down to it.

For most extinct species, what we see in the fossil record is actually the middle of a species' story. We typically don't find the
exact beginnings or precise endings of ancient species, although
paleontologists use terms like First or Last Appearance Dates to
connote when a species is first observed in the fossil record or when
it drops out of view. But First and Last Appearance Dates are ar-
bitrary markers in a species' evolutionary story; they tell us more
about the conditions that preserve fossils than they necessarily do
about when and how ancient species lived and died.

Consequently, we tend to tell a species' origin story not through
its evolutionary beginning but, rather, through its cultural one. We
use the discovery of a fossil species as the narrative point of "origin"

27. Morton, *Realist Magic,* 29.

to tell the story of a particular species. For long-extinct species, we read their species' stories as opening—for us, anyway—*in media res,* in the middle and at the moment of their discovery.

Each of those episodes—those beginnings, those middles, those endings—offers another matryoshka doll–like story nestled into an endling's ethos. This temporal depth—these multitudes of stories—make an endling more than just a character going extinct, more than just "dead." It folds them into an Anthropocene canon of stories; many endling extinction stories are only a generation or two removed from living memory.

In 2006, an international team of scientists working with the Wuhan Institute of Hydrobiology carried out an extensive survey along roughly one thousand miles of the Yangtze River in central China. The team was looking for baiji—*Lipotes vexillifer*—a freshwater dolphin endemic to river's unique ecosystem. Like its fellow river dolphins around the world, the baiji were characterized by long thin beaks filled with sharp teeth and by poor eyesight.

Over six weeks, from November to December of 2006, the team traveled down the river on two research vessels, from Yichang to the Three Gorges Dam to Shanghai and finally the Yangtze Delta before traversing their way back. Using optical instruments and underwater microphones, the scientists systematically and methodically tried to find any last remnant of the species that had lived in Yangtze River for millennia.

"We passed slowly between soggy mud banks heavy with wet grass and the skeletons of trees . . . in front of the ship everything faded into a grey void. It was completely silent. We stood vigilantly on deck, peering out into the blankness. Everything felt poised and expectant," British conservation biologist Samuel Turvey wrote of his experience on the 2006 survey, ". . . and then, ahead of us, the end of the side-channel condensed out from the grey air. We had seen nothing."[28]

28. Turvey, *Witness to Extinction,* 176.

For thousands of years, people along the Yangtze have told stories about how the baiji came to be through poems, stories, and myths. The animals in these stories are mystical and mythical, entwining people and the river together; sometimes, in such tellings, the baiji is cast as a "river goddess." The majority of baiji stories invariably contain an element of metamorphosis—the river changed a person from one state of being (human) into another (baiji or porpoise).

The baiji remained unrecognized to the Western world until 1914, when seventeen-year-old American Charles Hoy shot one near Chenglingji, in a water channel connecting the Yangtze with Dongting Lake. Hoy cleaned the skull and some vertebrae, and then sent the bones back to the United States where they ended up at the Smithsonian Institution in Washington, D.C. (The Smithsonian was so impressed with Hoy's ability to procure "exotic" animals that the institution sent him to Australia a few years later to acquire specimens. Incidentally, Hoy died in 1922 from schistosomiasis from a flatworm he picked up from the Yangtze River.)

In the mid-century decades after the end of China's civil war, Chairman Mao's "Great Leap Forward" for the People's Republic emphasized industrialization on a gargantuan scale—with that came forest and habitat destruction, such as the large dams that were put along the Yangtze, which splintered fish and baiji populations. Local Chinese who lived along the Yangtze were starving, and baiji—like many of the river's animals—were a source of food.

The Yangtze Freshwater Dolphin Expedition in 2006 concluded that, although it was possible that they had missed one or two baiji, the species was likely to be extinct. The species was functionally extinct, in other words. In their scientific publication, the team pointed to unsustainable by-catch in local overfishing, habitat degradation, severe pollution, and noisy shipping lanes that interfered with the dolphins' sonar (the Yangtze is one of the world's busiest waterways and is home to more than 10 percent of the world's human population) as contributing factors to the baijis' extinction. New methods of fishing—like electrifying the waters—were catastrophic for baiji. Like many threatened and endangered animals, the story is sadly familiar. (The Chinese paddlefish [*Psephurus gladius*], for example, may have also become extinct along this same timeline for very similar reasons.)

In 1980, one of the last few baiji was rescued from the river, given the name 淇淇 (Qi Qi—pronounced *chee chee* in English), and taken to the Wuhan Institute of Hydrobiology. Qi Qi was part of conservation efforts to save the *Lipotes vexillifer* species, and Qi Qi became a bit of a national celebrity. In 1986, two additional baiji—a female called Zhen Zhen and an unnamed male—were brought to the Institute. The male died within a few weeks of his arrival at the Institute, but the Institute had hopes that Zhen Zhen would be able to mate with Qi Qi. She died, however, before reaching sexual maturity.

And then there was just one. Just Qi Qi who, by some accounts, became so used to humans that he enjoyed being hauled out of the water. Almost all existing photographs of the baiji species are of Qi Qi in captivity in Wuhan. When Qi Qi died in 2002—of diabetes and old age—he had been in captivity for twenty-two years. His funeral was broadcast on national television.[29]

What are the stories of endlings like Benjamin and Qi Qi about?

Extinction, of course. They're about how millions of years of evolutionary history ends. And hubris. They're about ignorance, negligence, misogyny, colonialism. Name the sin and the odds are good that we can find it in the thylacine and river dolphin stories somewhere. They're stories about how we humans took species and we spent them. Carelessly.

We have the beginnings of one million endlings in the making—some species are closer to their endling than others, some critically so. As of 2022, species like the Sumatran rhino are estimated to have fewer than eighty individuals; the Māui dolphin has fifty-four; in the southeast United States, there are eighteen to twenty-five known

29. Fuller, *Lost Animals*.

red wolves in the wild (235 to 250 are in human care); there are fewer than ten vaquita individuals that live in the northern Gulf of California; there are three or four Yangtze softshell turtles in China and Vietnam.[30] (Most of these examples have decreased in their tiny population size between drafts of this book and counts had to be updated during the editing process. It is safe to assume that by the time you read this, we will be ever closer to endlings for these species.) Whether we name the individual or not—whether we know the individual or not—all of these relict species will come to their eventual endling and go extinct. To say nothing of the extinct of thousands of species that we haven't even yet "discovered" or named. We're writing a new set of endling stories, each one its own nested set of stories about beginnings and endings.

Fatu and Najin—northern white rhinos—are perhaps, the most famous "almost-endlings" in the world. They're a subspecies of white rhinoceros that once ranged across central Africa, including parts of Uganda, Sudan, and the Democratic Republic of the Congo. Decades of poaching have decimated the northern white rhino population as their horns are sold at astronomical prices on black markets.

For the past decade or so, we've marked the decline of the northern white rhino one individual at a time. The last white rhinos spent most of their lives in Europe, not Africa. In 2009, four individuals— Sudan, Suni, Najin, and Fatu—were sent to the Ol Pejeta Conservancy in Kenya from the Dvůr Králové Zoo in the Czech Republic. (The Dvůr Králové Zoo has an extensive and successful breeding program for African ungulates.) Suni, a male, died in 2014. Sudan died in 2018. Now Fatu and Najin live under armed guard at Ol Pejeta

---

30. Gander, "10 Species Still around That Might Not Be in 2030"; Kaitlin Solimine, "World's Largest Freshwater Turtle Nearly Extinct," https://www.nationalgeographic.com/animals/article/130703-china -yangtze-giant-softshell-turtle-animal-science; Crane, "Chasing the World's Most Endangered Turtle"; CeCe Sieffert, email interview with author, January 27, 2022; Chris Lasher, email interview with author, January 27, 2022; Lindsay Wickman, email interview with author, January 30, 2022.

Conservancy, like Sudan did, to protect them from poachers. "Sudan is an extreme symbol of human disregard for nature," Jan Stejskal, director of international projects at the Dvůr Králové Zoo said, upon the rhinoceros's death in 2018. "He survived extinction of his kind in the wild only thanks to living in a zoo."[31]

One of the ways that the stories of endlings are changing is how they are told to connect with their audiences. To make it personal. Certainly, this was true when Sudan died on March 19, 2018, and headlines around the world tolled for the ever closer, ever inevitable extinction of the northern white rhino. What did I do the day that he died? Looking back at my calendar, I went rock climbing. I picked up a prescription at the pharmacy. I was working on a couple of freelance articles and thinking about a new book project. And, then, the next day, I read in the *New York Times* that Sudan had died. Sudan's death—another reminder of the northern white rhinoceros's coming fate—made everything else seem downright banal. Time will tell who the northern white rhino endling will be.

"Last individuals—like Lonesome George, Martha the Passenger Pigeon, and Benjamin the Thylacine—continue to be central to the way in which popular commentary represents extinction," philosopher Thom Van Dooren offers. "These last individuals come to stand in for their whole species and sometimes the broader fact and possibility of extinction, in a way that lends persuasive power, but also creates important historical and ethical distortions."[32]

What can the stories of endlings and almost-endlings do, here in the twenty-first century, if species keep going extinct and will for the foreseeable future?

Today, we might like to tell ourselves that we tell endling stories as an act of memorializing. Perhaps even penance. Conceivably, we tell stories about endlings as proof that we're repentant about

31. Rachel Nuwer, "Sudan, the Last Male Northern White Rhino, Dies in Kenya," *The New York Times,* March 20, 2018, https://www.nytimes.com /2018/03/20/science/rhino-sudan-extinct.html.

32. Van Dooren, "Extinction," 173–74.

the harm that we humans have caused, with hope that, maybe, we could do a little better. Perhaps telling and retelling endling stories is about contrition; perhaps it's catharsis. We've learned our lesson, we would like to tell ourselves, and we'll be more careful in the future.

Other species—other endlings—might beg differ.

2. Extinctions and Endings: Celia the Ibex and Lonesome George the Tortoise

SEVEN MINUTES.

For seven minutes, on July 30, 2003, scientists bought an extinct taxon back to life for the first time in human history. Using cells that had been collected and cryogenically preserved from Celia, the last Pyrenean ibex, an international team of scientists based in Aragón, Spain, managed to clone her, roughly two hundred kilometers from the where her species had existed for tens of thousands of years. (The method was similar to how scientists cloned Dolly the sheep several years earlier.)

For seven minutes, this ibex—this living, triumphant feat of biological techno-wizardry—seemed to prove that extinction wasn't completely, totally, and irrevocably forever. That it might, *just might,* be possible to countermand the centuries of poor decisions we humans have made that put species in peril. If we could clone endangered or extinct species in a laboratory, the idea went, it might be possible to bring those species back to life. And if we could do this with an ibex from the Pyrenees, what about other endangered or extinct species? A northern white rhino? A wooly mammoth, even? *Jurassic Park* was only a beginning.

For seven minutes, after experiments that used hundreds of reconstructed embryos and dozens of failed embryo transfers, scientists produced a living, breathing Pyrenean ibex. For seven minutes its heart beat, its blood pumped, its synapses fired. For seven minutes, science fiction was reality. And then, in the same amount time that it takes to cook a pot of pasta, *Capra pyrenaica pyrenaica* went extinct for a second time when that clone died.

To date, de-extinction has not been repeated.

The Pyrenean ibex—*Capra pyrenaica pyrenaica*—was, technically, one of four subspecies of Iberian ibex, two of which are still alive today. (Another subspecies, the Portuguese ibex, went extinct in the late 1800s from overhunting.) Tracing the evolutionary history of Iberian ibex is a bit tricky, but fossils from the Upper Pleistocene suggest that an ancestor to the Pyrenean ibex moved into the Iberian Peninsula at the beginning of Europe's last glacial period somewhere between 120,000 and 80,000 years ago, eventually reaching southern France and the Pyrenees where it evolved into *C. pyrenaica pyrenaica* around 18,000 years ago.[1] Ibex even appear in a plethora of Upper Pleistocene cave paintings from sites in Spain and Portugal, mixed into art panels with other animals like aurochs (a European wild ox that went extinct in the 1600s), bison, mammoths, deer, and horses. Although archaeologists debate the artistic, epistemic, and social meanings of the painted ibex, the animal was inexorably part of the area's ecology and landscape. Pleistocene artists recognized that.[2]

The Pyrenean ibex were well adapted to extreme cold and snow of winter in the Pyrenees; ibex had short, brown fur and males had dark brown-black fur from their shoulders to their hooves. The ibex preferred a rocky scrubland habitat, making the cliffs and mountain outcrops of places like the Pyrenean massif an ideal habitat. (Aragón's Ordesa Valley, carved out by glaciers 65,000 years

1. García-González, "New Holocene *Capra Pyrenaica* (Mammalia, Artiodactyla, Bovidae) Skulls from the Southern Pyrénées."
2. Bicho et al., "The Upper Paleolithic Rock Art of Iberia."

ago, served as the last bastion of the animals' fragmentary habitat.)[3] Both ibex sexes had horns, and the horns of the male ibex were long, curved, and, particularly in the nineteenth century, were prized as hunting trophies by hunters across Europe.

Humans have been hunting ibex in the Pyrenees for millennia—the problem for the ibex and its subspecies was overhunting. The earliest published account of the ibex was Gaston Phébus's *Livre de la Chasse* ("Hunting Book") published between 1387 and 1389, dedicated to Philip II, Duke of Burgundy. "The ibex challenges the hunter from the heights of his rocky perch," Phébus writes, emphasizing the inhospitable terrain and elusive nature of the animal. "Following him is impossible: in a few dizzy leaps, from traverse to traverse, he disappears out of range of arrow or stone."[4]

The ibex had—has—many names. In Aragonese and Spanish, it's a *bucardo;* a *herc* in Catalan; a *bouquetin* in French. In the centuries that followed the publication of *Livre de las Chasse,* the ibex—thanks to its iconic horns and elusive presence—became an internationally sought-after trophy, particularly among nobility who owned large expanses of land or summer homes in the area. (Some historians estimate that the bucardo became extinct in Basque country and Catalonia as early as the mid- to late eighteenth century.[5]) By the nineteenth century, hunting bucardos become linked to international, European bourgeois trophy hunting, spurred on in popularity by the reputation of the elusive animal.

This is where the bucardo becomes a different sort of overhunting story. Unlike the thylacines in Tasmania—animals that were feared and actively hunted with the intent to exterminate them—bucardos were hunted with a different intent. The more the bucardo was

3. The history and story of Celia builds upon conversations with Adam Searle, a cultural geographer, and his publications. Searle has spent years conducting ethnographic research tracing the ibex's footsteps in the Pyrenees. Searle, "Spectral Ecologies."

4. Searle, "Hunting Ghosts," 520.

5. Searle, 521.

hunted, the more elusive it became, and the more hunters sought
the animal as a test of hunting prowess. It was like the bucardo became an elusive ghost in the Pyrenees—its presence known, felt, and
sought after, but its individuals rarely encountered. (Geographer
Adam Searle points out that this an example of what the French
philosopher Jacques Derrida called "hantologie"—the persistence
of elements from the past.[6]) By 1900, there were fewer that one
hundred Pyrenean ibex left.[7]

Hunting the bucardo was officially prohibited in the 1913, and in
1918 Parque Nacional de Ordesa y Monte was founded to protect
its habitat. The goal was to stabilize and grow the bucardo population and bring the species back from the brink of extinction.
Conservation efforts were halted by both the Spanish Civil War
(1936–1939) as well as the decades of the Francoist dictatorship
that followed. By the time ecologists completed their first extensive
survey of the bucardo population in the national park in 1995, there
were only three female bucardos in the Ordesa valley.

To facilitate a larger ibex gene pool—which in turn could help
create a robust ibex herd—conservationists opted to try to hybrid-
ize the bucardo with other Pyrenean ibex to expand the bucardos'
genetic diversity. In January 1996, ecologists managed to cage-trap
one of the remaining bucardo females; she was kept in captivity
with Iberian ibex males to attempt to crossbreed, but she died of
illnesses associated with captivity and inbreeding after ten months
without having reproduced.

Eventually, in December 1996—after a tiresome political struggle
to obtain governmental permissions—two fertile Iberian ibex males
of the different subspecies were released by helicopter with radio-
tracking collars in the hopes that they would mate with the last
bucardo. But the population of bucardo—or what would have been
bucardo hybrids—did not increase. (Incidentally, the two introduced

6. Searle, "Spectral Ecologies."
7. Church and Regis, *Regenesis*.

males died. However, one of the males, nicknamed Correcaminos—
"road runner"—lived in the park for thirteen years, thus suggesting
that the bucardos' ecological niche might be successfully filled by a
different ibex subspecies, although opinions about the idea of such
ecological "success" differed.) By 1999, there was only one Pyrenean
ibex left—Celia.[8]

Celia was successfully trapped on April 20, 1999, tranquilized, and
a clipping from one of her ears was taken; genetic material offers an
archive of information to scientists for sequencing an organism's
genome, studying genetic diversity of a species, and, potentially, see-
ing how those elements change over time. Celia's genetic material
was cryogenically preserved with a sense of particular urgency, as
obtaining her cells while she was alive offered the best possibility—
the best last resort—that she could be cloned after she was dead.

It wasn't long after Celia had been designated as the Pyrenean
ibex endling that she died. On January 6, 2000, she was crushed by
a falling fir tree. Park rangers recovered her body, a necroscopy of
the body was completed. Her genetic material was already stored
in a laboratory in Zaragoza, Aragón; her remains were subsequently
reassembled by taxidermists. With the extinction of the bucardo,
cloning became the last possibility for having a living bucardo on
earth.

Celia's cloning was a complicated process. Embryos were trans-
ferred to either a pure Spanish ibex subspecies or a hybrid of a
Spanish ibex male and a domestic goat; some pregnancies termi-
nated spontaneously. For all the efforts, the only "success" lasted
seven minutes. "One bucardo female weighing 2.6k was obtained
alive, without external morphological abnormalities," the team reports in its scientific paper published six years later. "Although the
newborn displayed a normal cardiac rhythm as well as other vital
signs at delivery (i.e., open eyes, mouth opening, legs and tongue
movements), it suffered from severe respiratory distress after de-

8. Searle, "Spectral Ecologies."

livery and died some minutes later."[9] A subsequent necropsy revealed a lung pathology.

In their publication, the authors describe the potential efficacy of hybrid foster mothers for gestating embryos of cloned animals but acknowledge that cloning endangered or extinct species is perhaps best understood as a last, desperate attempt to keep living individuals of these species. More than twenty years after her death, Celia's material remains are geographically dispersed—pieces of her skin, bones, and genetic material are scattered and now act as points to triangulate the story of Celia, the endling.

"It was Wednesday, July 30, 2003, a turning point in the history of biology. For on that date, all at once, extinction was no longer forever," synthetic biologist George Church and science writer Ed Regis triumphantly declared to their readers in *Regenesis: How Synthetic Biology Will Reinvent Nature and Ourselves*.[10] (Synthetic biology combines physical and genetic engineering with evolutionary biology—among other disciplines—to actively design or redesign organisms with new, "useful," human-centric purposes.) For many techno-acolytes, Church among them, Celia's cloning was a "success"—the experiments showed that de-extinction was, technically, possible. (Saving frozen tissue samples—in places like San Diego Zoo Wildlife Alliance's "Frozen Zoo" or The Frozen Ark in the United Kingdom—are ways to archive these animals.) What's technically *possible,* however, has not translated into herds of ibex in the Pyrenees; the species is just as extinct as it was prior to the world's only de-extinction event.

"What might it mean, then, for ibex to return?" geographer Adam Searle ponders. "These animals are not bucardo—rather, they are ecological and cultural proxies. The ways in which they are understood to *belong* in the Pyrenees is not straightforward, but shaped by myriad issues linked to tourism, hunting, and na-

9. García-González, "New Holocene Capra Pyrenaica (Mammalia, Artiodactyla, Bovidae) Skulls from the Southern Pyrénées," 1029–30.

10. Church and Regis, *Regenesis.,* pp 136.

tionalism, among others."[11] In other words, even if another ibex is cloned in another lab, it will never be a bucardo—that moment is gone, as well as the species.

Today, conservation efforts for the other two subspecies have created cautious optimism about ibex populations rebounding. In a different sort of de-extinction story, populations of ibex—primarily western Spanish ibex—have been introduced into the French Pyrenees; fall 2020, for example, saw numerous ibex kids born in France where the ibex had previously been found but hunted to local extinction. This ibex is a twenty-first-century animal, filling the niche of the extinct Pyrenean ibex—a ghost-like, elusive species that became real. The population now stands at roughly four hundred individuals.[12]

Extinction, of course, like all endling stories are. This particular endling story is also about de-extinction and the hope that we hang on finding a technological fix for addressing threatened species. It's about valiant efforts at conservation, official protections, legislations, habitat sanctuaries—all of which were too little, too late for the species. Although Celia's death doesn't have the grim callousness of other endlings' deaths—she wasn't left out in the cold to die, for example—her death marks an ending in the *Capra pyrenaica pyrenaica* species narrative.

The story of Celia the endling has become synonymous with twenty-first century de-extinction efforts. And de-extinction is about heroic, grandiose—some might say futile?—attempts to roll back decades—centuries, really—of decisions in the name of "doing everything" in an attempt to reverse extinction.

11. Searle, "Anabiosis and the Liminal Geographies of De/Extinction," 13.

12. Searle, "Hunting Ghosts"; Agence France-Presse, "Ibex Population Thrives in French Pyrenees a Century after Being Wiped Out," *The Guardian,* September 3, 2020, https://www.theguardian.com/environment /2020/sep/04/ibex-population-thrives-in-french-pyrenees-a-century-after -being-wiped-out.

But that endling telling is just one matryoshka layer of Celia's biography. In April 2018, Adam Searle arrived in the village of Torla in Aragón to explore and piece together the story of Celia as part of his graduate research into de-extinction and political ecology. Searle wanted to study an endling, like Celia—and to record what stories people tell about her and her fellow bucardos.

"I was in a bar in Huesca, and I asked Pablo, an environmental activist from Ecologistas en Acción (Environmentalists in Action) to explain his feelings toward the bucardo and its clone," Searle describes. "We spoke about it for a while. So how did you feel when Celia died, I asked him, which I thought nothing of. 'Celia? Well, I don't know, that's not her name to anyone from here . . . it's a name from outside, from the scientists who tried to clone her . . . her name is Laña, which comes from the local language of Aragonese, a name for a forest clearing in the Pyrenees.'"[13]

Searle described to me how this exchange was a lightbulb moment for him and his research. In the last two decades of media surrounding the death of the ibex, the discussion has been about Celia the ibex, not Laña the bucardo. Why? In his interview with Searle, Pablo joked that it was because the letter ñ doesn't exist in English, so perhaps the scientists at the lab in Zaragoza wanted to use a name that would be accessible, particularly across the English-speaking scientific press. "I think of this as 'A Tale of Two Bucardo,'" Searle explained to me as we chatted about his research and endlings. "Both Celia and Laña connect with how we think about extinction and loss. There are many, many ways to talk about this animal and its afterlives."[14]

"Celia" and her narrative have become a product of the chapter in the ungulate's life where she was an endling, a clone, and then the world's only double extinction. In this story, Celia is unlucky, tragic, lost, alone, *la última* of her kind. (An endling of this trope is

13. Searle, "A Tale of Two Bucardo."
14. Adam Searle, Zoom interview with author, June 18, 2021.

very strong in David Quammen's *The Song of the Dodo,* where he asks his readers to imagine the last, lonely, little old lady dodo bird at the end of her species.) In this sort of telling, an endling like Celia draws heavily in popular imagination and presentation to what environmental scholar Ursula Heise calls a "gender fiction" involving "elegiac tropes of the bereaved mother and wife, as well as that of the elderly lady with health problems."[15] It's much more tragic, it invokes so much more pathos, for the story of an endling to be told as a sad old lady ibex who died, alone, without family to mourn her.

"Laña," on the other hand, was the name and persona that people in Torla had ascribed to the bucardo in her life and memorialized after her death. The bucardo museum was founded in April 2013, amidst a whirlwind of discussion about possibly trying to clone Celia—that is, Laña—again. The museum, which successfully fought to curate Laña's taxidermied remains, was emphatic in its commitment to the last bucardo being remembered *in situ.* That she should be "home" and visible to the community. "Being here, in Torla, meant that the bucardo could find new meanings outside the realm of technoscience," Searle notes. "Laña lives on."[16]

Animal stories occupy a vital literary and cultural niche. The twentieth-century anthropologist Claude Lévi-Strauss commented that animals were *"bons à penser"*—"good to think." (Sometimes translated as "good to think with"—a translation that sounds less messy in English.) We tell animal stories to tell ourselves about the natural world, of course. We also tell animal stories to talk about our human selves with the comfortable narrative distance that anthropocentrism offers.[17]

Humankind has a long tradition of telling stories about animals. Step back in time to the cave walls of Pleistocene-era humans

15. Heise, *Imagining Extinction,* 38.
16. Searle, "A Tale of Two Bucardo."
17. Levi-Strauss, *Totemism,* 89.

around the world, and we find a plethora of animals painted and inscribed—visual animal stories as recorded and encountered by us today spanning tens of thousands of years. From fables to folk stories to fairy tales, humans tell stories about animals in a flurry of forms and have for millennia.

Why?

"Folk tales talk about human struggles and troubles. They carry universal truths of the human condition," anthropologist Gessica Sakamoto Martini explained to me. Sakamoto Martini's own work examines how the Cinderella story has changed, morphed, and transformed over time. "If someone feels powerless, then there is a fairy tale about that girl, or boy, embarking on a journey to reclaim personal power and agency. There is something deep about the stories, perhaps that's why they were able to survive for so long."[18]

As a profoundly anthropocentric species, animal stories are a way for us to tell stories about humans while deemphasizing the human narrator. "As a rule, animal tales have little in common with the real lives and ways of animals," famed folklore and literary scholar Vladimir Propp notes. "Animals are usually no more than conditional bearers of the action."[19] In other words, in the Western tradition of animal storytelling, giving animals certain characteristics, actions, and purposes often just makes them thinly veiled symbols of our own human foibles, vices, and limitations. (Some folklore scholars suggest that animal stories have helped transmit knowledge about animals that could potentially cause harm to humans and domesticated animals; in such instances, folktales would be important means of transmitting what might formally be called "folk-zoological knowledge."[20]) It's into this familiar literary niche of animal stories that we've thrust many endlings.

18. Gessica Sakamoto Martini, Zoom interview with author, February 14, 2022.

19. Propp and Zipes, *The Russian Folktale,* 286.

20. Nakawake and Sato, "Systematic Quantitative Analyses Reveal the Folk-Zoological Knowledge Embedded in Folktales."

"In Aristotelian poetics, the notion of character is secondary, entirely subordinated to the notion of plot," literary theorist Roland Barthes argues. "There can be fables without characters, according to Aristotle, but there cannot be characters without fables."[21] This question—the relationship between fable and characters—is at the very heart of endlings' stories. Does the sixth mass extinction simply form such a powerful plot that it hardly matters which characters tell it? Or do endlings as characters exist, at the ready, able to slot into whatever sort of extinction narrative that we want? Either way, those familiar elements of narrative theory—those building blocks of stories described by Propp, Lévi-Strauss, and others—are inescapably at play.

Within various genres, there are a plethora of rhetorical and literary devices at work in endling stories. Devices like irony ("the expression of one's meaning by using language that normally signifies the opposite"[22]) and poetic justice ("the fact of experiencing a fitting or deserved retribution for one's actions"[23]), for example, can add layers of depth and meaning to increase an audience's emotional response. Such devices, along with their literary cousins of metaphors and analogies, are ways for endling stories to resonate with their contemporary audiences, conveying a narrator's meaning with the ultimate goal of persuading the audience toward the intended pathos of the stories. They are particularly effective at provoking an emotional response, and what are endling stories if not stories that we have steeped in emotion?

Ultimately, animal stories are about mediating the relationship between humans and nature, with nonhuman characters as the guide. Philosopher Kim TallBear points out that when Western

21. Barthes and Duisit, "An Introduction to the Structural Analysis of Narrative," 256.

22. "Irony, n.," *OED Online*, accessed February 13, 2022, http://www .oed.com/view/Entry/99565.

23. "Poetic, adj. and n.," *OED Online,* February 13, 2022, http://www .oed.com/view/Entry/146532.

scholars "discover" alternative way of describing relationships with nonhumans, they ought to be aware that "indigenous peoples have never forgotten that nonhumans are agential beings engaged in social relations that profoundly shape human lives."[24]

Aesop's fables might be the best-known example of Western animal stories that are supposed to teach readers a lesson. Like many sorts of stories, Aesop's fables have changed over the centuries, evolving in their telling and purpose, growing in their connections to audiences. For example, in their original tellings, the animals in Aesop's fables were used to justify the killing or exploiting of other, weaker animals. A hawk that seizes a nightingale, for example, or a wolf that captures a sheep.[25] Interestingly, there are examples of contemporary science finding consistencies with animal behavior described in the fables; for instance, the is ample evidence that many corvid species, like crows, are capable tool-users and would have been able to raise the water level in a pitcher by adding pebbles to it, as Aesop describes. "We now know that modern science supports the behaviour of Aesop's crow," zoologist Jo Wimpenny points out in *Aesop's Animals,* "and while we don't know if Aesop had ever witnessed such behaviour in person, it is probable that his existing knowledge about these birds influenced his choice of animal in this fable."[26]

Today, Aesop's fables are generally regarded as children's stories, with easily identifiable and accessible morals, like "slow and steady wins the race" or "once bitten, twice shy." Anthropologist John Hartigan Jr. points out that the fable—as a literary genre—is used to "preform the most basic of cultural concerns: the transmissibility of experience, observation, and thought."[27] But animal fables have always been told under the narrative auspice that we humans could

24. TallBear, "An Indigenous Reflection on Working beyond the Human/Not Human."

25. Clayton, "Aesop, Aristotle, and Animals."

26. Wimpenny, *Aesop's Animals,* 56.

27. Hartigan, *Aesop's Anthropology,* 54.

learn something about ourselves, our place in nature, and the nature of humankind through the fables' telling. We use the animals to teach us to be better humans; not to be better nonhumans.

"[Aesop's] fables are an argument that other species are worthy of attention for more than their functional uses, because we may be able or need to learn something from them," Hartigan argues. "This mode of thought . . . is never very far from the allegorical. For naturalism, this may be abhorrent, but for cultural anthropologists, this is rather a reminder of what we've long known about any forms of social analysis: they cannot be rendered without the inflections of myth and meaning, specifically for us, as humans."[28]

It's hard to look at a story like Benjamin's, Qi Qi's, or Lonesome George's, though, and not wonder if Aesop wrote fables here in the Anthropocene, what would he make of endling animal stories? Do we tell them to learn a lesson? To remember the last of a species? To shape how we'll talk about the future's inevitable endlings?

Or something more?

The story of Celia—Laña—and all endlings hinges on extinction. Species gave us a narrative arc for endlings; extinction gives us their end. So what is extinction, exactly?

In contemporary biology, ecology, and paleontology, scientists use "extinction" to talk about the death of a population of breeding organisms. Today, extinction is a basic tenet of contemporary scientific thinking—species evolve, they live, and eventually they will, probably, go extinct. An estimated 99.9 percent of all species that have ever existed are extinct. Extinct species number in the billions.

Although the fossil record shows that extinction is part of life on earth in deep time, current extinction rates are much higher than their precursors in the fossil records, due to environmental degradation, habitat endangerment, black market smuggling, and countless human decisions that put millions and millions of species in a jeopardy that they would not have been in otherwise.

28. Hartigan, 53.

In Western science, the concept of extinction was formalized
by the early nineteenth-century French naturalist Georges Cuvier.
Working with fossils at the Muséum National d'Histoire Naturelle
in Paris (National Museum of Natural History), Cuvier published
formal, anatomical descriptions of a mammoths, mastodons, and
giant ground sloths, proposing that giant fossil bones belonged to
species of quadrupeds that were no longer alive on earth. These
bones "seem to me," Cuvier said, "to prove the existence of a world
previous to ours, destroyed by some kind of catastrophe."[29] These
bones, Cuvier argued, belonged to animals that were *éteint, disparu,*
or *mort.* Organisms that were no longer here on earth—*l'extinction.*
Extinct.

It's worth noting that, initially, "extinction" was a far from uni-
versally accepted idea. The third American president and naturalist Thomas Jefferson (1743–1826), for example, famously believed
that it was impossible for a species to go extinct. "In the present
interior of our continent there is surely space and range enough
for elephants and lions, if in that climate they could subsist; and for
the mammoth and megalonyxes who may subsist there," Jefferson
wrote in a report to the American Philosophical Society on February
10, 1797. "Our entire ignorance of the immense country to the
West and North-West, and of its contents, does not authorise us
so say what is does not contain."[30] Jefferson was convinced that
mammoths—mastodons, technically—were out there in the to-be-
discovered American wilderness and specifically instructed the
famous explorers Meriwether Lewis and William Clark to see if
they couldn't find one during their 1803–1806 expedition of the
then–Louisiana Purchase and Pacific Northwest. Needless to say,
Lewis and Clark returned *sans* proboscidean.[31]

29. Kolbert, "The Lost World."
30. Thomas Jefferson, "Memoir on the Megalonyx, [10 February
1797]," accessed February 27, 2022, http://founders.archives.gov/documents
/Jefferson/01-29-02-0232.
31. Giaimo, "Thomas Jefferson Built This Country on Mastodons";
Bressan, "Thomas Jefferson's Patriotic Monsters."

Extinction is a word that we use easily today, but the word itself predates its current scientific convention. In the early seventeenth century, long before Cuvier's work with fossils, "extinction" applied to living organisms—beings—like human families or animal species. Rather poetically, linguist Kate Wiles explained to me, this Middle English use of "extinction" was derived from the Latin verb *extinguere,* meaning "to quench, extinguish, kill" and was typically used to describe flames, like candles, going out. For centuries, writers, artists, and philosophers borrowed heavily from this idea to intertwine the metaphor of flame and life. ("Out, out brief candle . . ." and the like.)[32]

Extinguish was also used to mean "to put a total end to, do away with, blot out of existence," which offers a fairly direct root for the modern sense of how we use *extinct.* (In 1603, for example, English writer Henry Crosse observed, "Two contraries, cannot ioyntly hold possession, but one will vtterly extinct the other." Likewise, in 1615, the English poet and translator George Sandys wrote "This late mightie Empire [of the Turks] extinguish in Ægypt by the Mamalucks," in his essay "A Relation of a Journey.")[33] It's from the verb *to extinct* that the adjective *extinct* was derived. From the late fifteenth century, *extinct*-as-an-adjective was used in all the same ways as the verb—to put out a flame; to have lost passion, life, or hope; of a volcano that has ceased eruption; and, of course, people who were cut off and blotted out of existence. The Caxton printing of the "Golden Legende" (Lives of Saints) of 1483, for example, states that "All [the people] were . . . deed and extinct."[34] The use of "extinct" or "extinction" shifted to include more than just a single individual and expanded to notions of race and familial lines—such that "race" was understood and used in the late seventeenth century. Daniel Defoe, in the *Life of Robinson*

32. Kate Wiles, email interview with author, March 25, 2021.
33. OED, s.v., "extinction."
34. Wiles interview.

Crusoe (1719), for example, writes: "My Father was dead, and my Mother, and all the Family extinct."[35]

And it's this narrative pathos of a lineage being snuffed out that—directly or indirectly—offered a draw for the natural history community, decades later, to describe how entire species of animals could no longer be alive on earth. The idea that extinction is infused with narrative and metaphor is a powerful driver of biodiversity and wildlife conservation movements. We care about species going extinct—as evidenced by a plethora of books, documentaries, fundraising for awareness—because we have a tragic story. Extinction creates emotional stakes for us humans to care about nonhuman species.

"The noun *extinction* was, from the mid-sixteenth century, also used to talk about the quenching of fire or light," medieval linguist Kate Wiles explained to me. "*Extinction* was also adopted by scientific communities, used in physics to talk about radiation, beams of light, x-rays, and, of course, fossil species, which might be why we associate the concept less with candles and hope now."[36]

Fast-forward two hundred years since Cuvier, and the question isn't so much: "Do species go extinct?" (Short answer: "yes.") The more pertinent question is: "How and when do species become extinct?" (Short answer: "It depends.") For endlings, the question is, "Is extinction the end point of endling stories or could it be a narrative frame for endling characters?"

Narratively, extinction is a point of termination. Endlings offer a set of stories—poignant, wrenching stories—for us humans to tell ourselves and each other about the extinctions we've caused. An endling provides a character that offers a moral or lesson about why things like habitat loss, environmental degradation, hybridization, and climate change are so weighty.

Endlings—as characters, as organisms, as beings—also pull from

35. OED, s.v., "extinction."
36. Wiles interview.

a plethora of other types of stories, like myths, folk stories, and fairy tales, that we humans have told for centuries about how to process loss, hubris, guilt, and ruin. In Old Norse mythology, for example, ecological catastrophe plays a big part in stories like Ragnarok, when the apocalypse will be preceded by a terrible three-year winter, submersion of the earth in floods, and the destruction of everything.[37] (After Ragnarok, the story goes, all will eventually be reborn.) Although Ragnarok isn't about individual species becoming extinct, it does frame a kind of universal mass extinction event—perhaps not unlike how we've framed species loss and climate change here in the twenty-first-century Anthropocene.

Consciously or unconsciously, how we tell stories about endlings draws from literature where we think about being alone or the last. The most compelling literary parallel for endlings, however, draws from a tradition in Old English where poets would often reflect on ruined or empty places and imagine the people who once inhabited them. (As *endling* is an English, Western-based word and concept, it follows that it would draw so specifically from a Western literary canon.) Most of the poets, philosophers, and writers who were engaged with the theme of extinction—"life extinguished"—were doing so through Christian philosophical and religious contexts about the end of the world.

In the Old English poem *Beowulf,* we see the emergence of a proto-endling-like character when the "last survivor" ruminates about what it means to be . . . well, the last. The last warrior, the last fighter, the last one of his kind. The audience knows this person only as someone who has treasure, wealth, and power, but no one is around for him to share it with. What is it, the survivor ponders, to be the end of his lineage, his culture, his people? In Maria Dahvana Headley's recent (2020) translation of *Beowulf,* the poem offers a particular relevance to the endlings of today as she opted to describe the death of the last survivor as an extinction.

37. Eleanor Parker, email interview with author, March 31, 2021.

Now there are no heroes, no soothing music,

. . .

We existed; now we're extinct.

And so the last survivor mourned, making his way

. . .

wandering the world woefully, until death came . . .[38]

Perhaps the most striking part of this is a narrative distance between himself and the audience, who "overhears" his lament.[39] The last survivor is an endling, in the same way we have come to create other, nonhuman endlings—distanced characters that we, as audience members, understand because we're living with characters like him in endling after endling after endling.

"In the context of *Beowulf,* which is so much about the rise and fall of kings and heroes, it's a reminder of the limitations of human power and wealth," medieval scholar Eleanor Parker explained to me over email. "The 'last survivor' there is left with all the treasures of his people, but they've become worthless once there's no one to use or exchange them, so all he can do is bury them. It's a 'dust to dust' kind of idea."[40] It's not too much of a stretch to see how endlings stories become stories of last survivors.

Stories that are framed as a "Last Survivor" often deal with tribal groups or kingdoms that have become "extinct," ("extinguished") and poets are often focused on using the material remains they've left behind (either ruined buildings, or objects like the treasure hoard in the *Beowulf,* for example) to prompt reflections on mortality, the transience of life and what it would mean for the human candle to go out. Medieval archaeologist David Petts is quick, however, to point out that while medieval poets might have framed their literature in this way, it isn't how contemporary researchers think

---

38. Headley, *Beowulf,* lines 2261–64, emphasis added.
39. Reynolds, "Beowulf's Poetics of Absorption."
40. Parker interview.

about loss and continuity in the past. "In archaeology, we don't talk about the 'death' of a culture or a civilization particularly. It rather smacks of outdated models of early societies which saw them composed of distinct, bounded entities like peoples and tribes that might be seen as 'dying,'" Petts explained to me. "Instead, today, the focus is much more on notions of transformation and continuity."[41] Perhaps looking for continuity and transformation could be new ways to evolve in endling storytelling.

Headley's use of the word *extinct* in her translation is striking—in no small part, because other no major translation of Beowulf uses that specific word in that specific, famous section. "Extinct" is wonderfully jarring to the reader. It feels so contemporary compared with the medieval world of the poem and so timely for her contemporary Anthropocene readers. Endlings and extinctions are fundamentally part of our world, today, but we've been telling stories about endlings for hundreds and hundreds of years as *Beowulf* attests.

It's hard to imagine an endling that is more famous than the twenty-first-century Pinta Island Galápagos tortoise Lonesome George. When George was found on the small island in the northern part of the Galápagos archipelago in 1971, *Chelonoidis abingdonii*—George's species—was thought to be long extinct from centuries of overhunting by buccaneers, whalers, and Galápagos settlers. (Prior to George, the last sighting of a Pinta Island tortoise had been by scientists in 1906.[42]) In 1959, the Ecuadorian government created the Galápagos National Park to protect tortoise habitats; conservation efforts today form a backbone of eco-tourism that draws hundreds of thousands of tourists to the islands to see their animals.[43]

41. David Petts, email interview with author, April 13, 2021.
42. Nicholls, *Lonesome George*.
43. "Galápagos Tortoises, Facts and Photos," https://www .nationalgeographic.com/animals/reptiles/facts/galapagos-tortoise; Turtle Conservation Coalition, "Turtles in Trouble: The World's 25+ Most

Lonesome George was more than one hundred years old when he died on June 24, 2012, at the park. "He was a favorite with tourists— famous not because he was the largest tortoise, nor the oldest of the animals who can live 150 to 200 years," geographer Elizabeth Hennessy points out in her history of the Galápagos tortoises. "George was famous because he was the last of his species."[44]

When Lonesome George died, the media emphasized how the tortoise was a cautionary tale, a reminder of how fragile species and ecosystems are, how much blame humans shoulder for causing extinctions. (Very Aesop-like.) "Mourning him was about mourning the history of human-caused extinction," Hennessy points out. "His story puts into stark relief the ways dominant human conceptions of nature have changed over the past centuries from God-given resources for human consumption to beings with whom we share an earth-bound history of evolution."[45]

Tissue and blood samples were collected from George after his death; they have been frozen and stored in Ecuador, for future conservation possibilities or tortoise breeding strategies. (Policymakers considered these pieces of Lonesome George cultural patrimony of Ecuador and declined to send the specimens to the cryogenic "Frozen Zoo" in San Diego, where samples from many endangered animals are kept.) Today, a taxidermied Lonesome George has returned to the Galápagos after five years—time that included an exhibition at the American Museum of Natural History in New York City—and now has been installed as part of an exhibit at the park's museum in the Galápagos, what some have wryly termed a "mau-

Endangered Tortoises and Freshwater Turtles" (IUCN SSC Tortoise and Freshwater Turtle Specialist Group, Turtle Conservancy, Turtle Survival Alliance, Turtle Conservation Fund, Conservation International, Chelonian Research Foundation, Wildlife Conservation Society, and Global Wildlife Conservation, 2018), https://www.iucn.org/content/turtles-trouble-worlds-25-most-endangered-tortoises-and-freshwater-turtles; Hennessy, *On the Backs of Tortoises*.

44. Hennessy, *On the Backs of Tortoises*, 6
45. Hennessy, 7, 15

soleum."[46] *Solitario Jorge* was a last survivor come home, standing sentinel, to tell his stories to people who will listen.

Millennia of literature and storytelling have shaped how we understand organisms like endlings. We understand (more or less) what it is for a species to be extinct. We understand (more or less) that endlings have a unique biological, historical, and cultural niche. We ought to consider—to acknowledge—how we continually give endlings these human stories.

We tell them through tropes that we know, through literary traditions that are familiar, through an anthropocentrism that would seem to affirm us as the storytellers. (How we tell the story of Lonesome George as a twenty-first century "last survivor;" like *Beowulf* but with a tortoise protagonist.) Such anthropocentrism, however, does not allow animals their own agency and forces every nonhuman into our an "idea that nonhuman animals also have a stake in challenging our anthropocentrism," philosopher Fiona Probyn-Rapsey argues. "Unless nonhuman voices on the matter of anthropocentrism are considered, our insights remain one sided and, well, anthropocentric."[47]

The question goes even deeper than just anthropocentrism. It forces us humans to reconsider our premise of our species' exceptionalism and the storytelling privilege that comes with it. Behaviors that we once thought were uniquely human are not as exclusive as we might have thought in the past. "We now have solid evidence of culture, morality, rationality, and even rudimentary forms of linguistic communication. The concept of death should also be counted among those characteristics to which we can no longer resort to convince us of how very special we are," philosopher Susana Monsó argues in *Aeon,* summarizing her research on how animals experience and understand death. "It is time to rethink human exceptionalism, and the disrespect for the natural world that comes with it."[48]

46. Jørgensen, *Recovering Lost Species in the Modern Age,* xvi.

47. Probyn-Rapsey, "Anthropocentrism," 48, 51

48. Monsó, "Animals Wrestle with the Concept of Death and Mortality."

If we listen to Qi Qi, Celia, Benjamin, Lonesome George, and other endlings, one wonders what their soliloquy—their "Lay of the Last Survivor"—might be. Would they describe being the lone surviving individual? Would they mourn their last-ness? Their extinction? Or would they tell us a new, different sort of endling story that we haven't even considered?

3. Charisma and Character: Incas the Carolina Parakeet, Turgi the Tree Snail, and Wood's Cycad

THEY SAID HE DIED OF A BROKEN HEART.

On Thursday, February 21, 1918, Incas, the last Carolina parakeet, passed away at the Cincinnati Zoo, surrounded by his keepers. A few months earlier, in the summer of 1917, Incas's companion of decades, the almost-endling parakeet Lady Jane, had died and by the keepers' accounts, Incas was bereft without her.[1]

Incas and Lady Jane were members of the only parrot (parakeet) species endemic to the United States—*Conuropsis carolinensis*. These were social, gregarious birds. Early accounts by European explorers in the sixteenth and seventeenth centuries mention the parrot, marveling at its colors—green, yellow, and red-orange. For centuries, the birds were seen in large flocks—sometimes hundreds of birds strong—living in moss-covered sycamores and cypress trees in river-bottom forests of the southern United States.

By the late nineteenth century, however, reports of parakeet sightings in the wild were rare, as their habitat was destroyed by agricultural practices that reshaped the parakeets' natural environments. The birds were considered pests to large plantation farms—

---

1. Fuller, *Lost Animals*, 73.

they ate crops—and they were exterminated as such. Some biologists have suggested that the hollow trees the birds used for nests were invaded by European honeybees, putting more pressure on the dwindling bird populations.[2] What's more, "the turn of the [twentieth-]century ladies' fashion fancied hats decorated with flashy feathers and sometimes even whole stuffed birds," environmental historian Mikko Saikku points out.[3] For over a century, all of these stresses built up for the species, meaning that there were fewer and fewer parakeets in shrinking habitats and that the species was moving closer to extinction.

In the mid-1880s, a consignment of sixteen parakeets arrived at the zoo in Cincinnati. Over the years, this endling flock of Carolina parakeets died off—none of the chicks that hatched at the zoo survived to adulthood—until just Incas and Lady Jane were left. Here and there, sightings of Carolina parakeets in the wild were reported, but none were verified.

When Incas the endling died, it was just a few cages over from where another endling—Martha, the very last passenger pigeon—had passed away four years prior.[4]

Dying of a broken heart is a story that has long permeated the art and literary worlds.

It's not much of a stretch, for example, to think of Incas and Lady Jane as an avian version of the Tristan and Isolde Arthurian legend. (Tristan and Isolde's story is that of two tragic lovers who share a forbidden passion; when Tristan dies, Isolde immediately dies of grief alongside him.) While such anthropomorphizing helps tell the story of the two birds, it doesn't have the narrative breadth to consider the centuries of habitat destruction and hunting pressures that the Carolina parakeet had faced, factors that caused the extinction of the species. What it does, however, is offer a relatable—

2. Cokinos, "The Carolina Parakeet Reminds Us to Do Better."
3. Saikku, "The Extinction of the Carolina Parakeet," 9.
4. Saikku; Fuller, *Lost Animals,* 73.

sentimental?—story for the deaths of the last two of these birds. This relatability, in turn, helps us tell some animal stories, like Incas and Lady Jane's, more easily than others.

This begs the question: What animals, what species, do we tell extinction stories about and why? Why do animals—well, certain animals—offer such compelling, charismatic endlings and endling stories? And why do other organisms, like plants and protozoa, not? At least, not yet?

Parrots, thylacines, rhinoceroses, ibex, river dolphins, and even parakeets—these are all animals that we might call charismatic in their popular appeal. These are all animals that are easy for we humans to anthropomorphize and rally behind. Charismatic animals offer a "sympathetic face" (or, in terms of storytelling, a sympathetic character) for public audiences. It's easy to want to save panda bears and elephants; it's harder to convince people to care as urgently about the critically endangered venomous Sahul reef snake.

In 2018, a team of conservation biologists determined that "the public"—such that they are—considered the following animals to be the top ten charismatic animals on the planet to be: tigers (*Panthera tigris*), lions (*Panthera. leo*), elephants (*Loxodonta africana, Loxodont cyclotis,* and *Elephas maximus*), giraffes (*Giraffa camelopardalis*), leopards (*Panthera. pardus*), pandas (*Ailuropoda melanoleuca*), cheetahs (*Acinonyx jubatus*), polar bears (*Ursus maritimus*), gray wolves (*Canis lupus*), and gorillas (*Gorilla beringei* and *Gorilla gorilla*).[5] They did point out that while invertebrates (like spiders and butterflies), cephalopods (like an octopus), and animals without fur did not rank—and often don't for conservation fundraising—there are many species that have a "local charisma" that impacts their own local conservation efforts.

Because charismatic animals—which we tend to associate with giant, furry megafauna—are often species in apex positions in their ecosystems (like wolves or big cats), it's easy to understand how and

5. Courchamp et al., "The Paradoxical Extinction of the Most Charismatic Animals," e2003997.

why their extinction would wreak havoc on their ecosystems. (For example, an apex predator can keep prey populations under control in an ecosystem.) Not only are they charismatic, such thinking goes, their ecological role is quite visible.

In conservation circles, charismatic animals are often "flagships" for other, less popular animals. While this notion doesn't carry much ecological weight—the way "umbrella" or "keystone" species does—it certainly matters within wildlife fundraising. "The flagship species approach is an enduring strategy in conservation," geographers Paul Jepson and Maan Barua point out, emphasizing that these charismatic animals "capture the attention of stakeholders and publics in ways that generate forms of support leading to positive conservation outcomes."[6]

And the cost? Is there a cost to species when we humans determine them to be "charismatic"?

"Some species can be the victims of their charisma, especially invertebrates which are not considered by the public as sensitive," biologists Frédéric Ducarme, Gloria Luque, and Franck Courchamp write. Which is to say that lots of rare and endangered species with a shape or color that strikes humans' fancy can be collected by tourists as souvenirs, or by local people to be sold to tourists as part of the "curios trade." This leads to rapid local extinctions of "charismatic" species. "This is especially the case of sessile beings like beautiful, endangered flowers (like the edelweiss *Leontopodium alpinum*), expensive edible mushrooms, or even sea stars and shellfishes," the three biologists point out. "For example, overfishing of the beautiful conch gastropod *Charonia tritonis* is often alleged as a probable cause for its prey's wrenching outbreaks, the coral-eating sea star *Acanthaster planci*."[7] In other words, the species we value—to save or to tell stories about—impacts other species in their ecosystems.

The living, working ways that we interact with animals have very real repercussions. It becomes self-reinforcing that the animals—

6. Jepson and Barua, "A Theory of Flagship Species Action," 95.
7. Ducarme, Luque, and Courchamp, "What Are 'Charismatic Species' for Conservation Biologists?," 8.

the endlings—whose stories we tell reinforce how we see animals. Such anthropocentrism (anthropomorphism, really) lets us ascribe characteristics and personas to animals that do not necessarily exist. (For example, snakes are not innately malevolent; monkeys are not always clever; crabs are not necessarily grumpy; snails are not proxies for sloth.) With so much species' extinctions—with so many endlings—which stories do we choose to tell?

Because it's easy to find literary themes and story tropes in charismatic animals, endlings that fit that sort of animal storytelling are given stories that are told and retold. When an endling is an animal of a species that humans "like," then the stories of Incas, Benjamin, or Celia easily resonate. "The fact that people tend to attach little sensitiveness to most invertebrates may also be seen as a limit to the use of charismatic species to help conservation programs," biologists Frédéric Ducarme, Gloria Luque, and Franck Courchamp point out.[8]

It's a cliché to point out that snails are slow, but the tiny tree snail species *Partula turgida* moved at less than two feet per year. Endemic to the Polynesian archipelago in the South Pacific (officially named Archipel de la Société; Tōtaiete mā in Tahitian; Society Islands in English), the *Partula* genus of tree snails lived and evolved in Polynesia over a million years.

Indeed, by the mid-twentieth century there were more than one hundred and twenty Polynesian tree snail species spread out over the archipelago. All *Partula* snail species are tiny—only a centimeter or two in size—and graze on algae from the surface of leaves in forests or consume dead vegetation, like decaying leaf stalks of hibiscus plants.[9] As detritivores, these snails are able to recycle nutrients in their ecosystems and assist with plants' respiration.

8. Courchamp et al., "The Paradoxical Extinction of the Most Charismatic Animals," 6.
9. Cunningham et al., "Mortality of Endangered Snails of the Genus Partula," 20.

However slowly the tree snails might have crawled in life, their extinction was swift and decisive. On Wednesday, January 1, 1996, the last Polynesian tree snail from the *Partula turgida* species died in the London Zoo. The snail—known as Turgi to the zoo's staff—was part of a captive breeding program to try to help that snail species, and others, found endemically in Polynesia. When Turgi died in London, he was almost 10,000 miles from home. A zoo spokesperson was quoted as saying the tombstone for Turgi would read "1.5 million years BC to January 1996."[10]

Partula snails have been culturally significant to Polynesia for centuries. Shells were used in making jewelry and ornamentation; islands had different species of *Partula,* each with its own distinct shell pattern lending themselves to different social networks along the islands. The snails were documented by English naturalist Joseph Banks, who was on board Captain James Cook's first voyage of the HMS *Endeavour.* For over a century, scientists have studied the adaptions and distributions of *Partula* species, because isolated habitats of the South Pacific islands provide an opportunity to study evolution, much like the Galápagos, as islands are epicenters of biodiversity and evolution. "They are the Darwin finches of the snail world," Paul Pearce-Kelly, a senior Zoological Society of London curator, offered of the various *Partula* species in a 2019 interview with *The Guardian.*[11]

Although habitat loss during the twentieth century put pressure on the tree snail species, the real extinction crisis for *Partula turgida* began when French authorities introduced giant African snails (*Lissachatina fulica* or *Achatina fulica*) to the islands for foodstuffs in 1967. (The islands are still part of French Polynesia, part of the

10. "1,500,000-Year Slow Road to Eternity Is Over for a Tiny Snail," *Evening Standard,* January 31, 1996, 12.

11. Robin McKie, "Precious Escargot: The Mission to Return Tiny Snails to Pacific Islands," *The Observer,* September 28, 2019, https://www .theguardian.com/environment/2019/sep/28/return-of-native-tiny-partula -snail-key-south-pacific-wildlife.

French Republic, thus subject to French authority.) The giant snails escaped, they bred, and they began to destroy local crops on the islands. In short, the introduced snails were out of control.

To combat the feral populations of giant African snails, authorities imported another, different carnivorous snail species—*Euglandina rosea,* or the rosy wolf snail—in the 1970s. Endemic to the southern United States, specifically Florida, the wolf snail was introduced to Hawai'i in 1955 to try and control a different outbreak of giant African snails; in that instance, the rosy wolf snail was responsible for the extinction of eight species of snail native to Hawai'i.[12] (The rosy wolf snail was known as "the Exocet of the snail world," the *Evening Standard* reported in 1996. The International Union for Conservation of Nature currently lists *Euglandina rosea* as one of the world's top one hundred most invasive species.[13]) Unsurprisingly, the rosy wolf snail quickly wreaked havoc on the Polynesian *Partula* species. Within a decade of its introduction, *Euglandina rosea* had wiped out twenty-seven endemic tree snail species. Today, scientists estimate that the rosy wolf snail is responsible for wiping out more than half of the *Partula* species that had once been spread over the entire archipelago.[14]

In 1991, Paul Pearce-Kelly and colleagues at the Zoological Society of London captured the last known individuals of *P. turgida* (in addition to other snails from similarly threatened *Partula* species, as they had on many collection trips) to create a breeding program for the snails at the London Zoo. By 1994, the snails in the program began dying, and veterinary pathologist Andrew Cunningham of the Institute of Zoology in London and then-parasitologist Peter Daszak

12. Kurt Auffenberg and Lionel Stange, "Snail-Eating Snails of Florida, Gastropoda," *University of Florida IFAS Extension,* Entomology and Nematology Department, Florida Cooperative Extension Service, Institute of Food and Agricultural Sciences, University of Florida, January 1, 2001, https://www.researchgate.net/publication/341887445_Snail-Eating_Snails _of_Florida_Gastropoda.

13. "1,500,000-Year Slow Road to Eternity Is Over for a Tiny Snail."

14. McKie, "Precious Escargot."

of Kingston University in Kingston-upon-Thames, England, began looking into possible causes. The population of captive *P. turgida* snails dwindled from 296 individuals to fewer than ten.

Postmortems on five of the tree snails showed that they were full of protozoan-like spores in their digestive glands and reproductive tracts, suggesting that a parasite had infected the snails. Daszak's analysis confirmed that the protozoa belonged to the phylum Microsporidia, known to infect aquatic snails; closer inspection revealed that the spores belonged to a new species of microsporidian in the genus *Steinhausia*. In a bit of evolutionary irony, *Steinhausia* did not appear to infect other land snails, and by killing off *P. turgida*, it seemed to have sealed its own fate—although irony means very little to Turgi or his fellow now-extinct snails.[15] "Only rarely has the cause of death been established for the last individual of a species and, when known, this usually was due to direct physical harm inflicted by humans," the scientific report published in *Conservation Biology* stated. "We believe that this is the first definitive record of an infectious disease causing a population to decline to the point of extinction—albeit this occurred in captivity and that the original decline in the wild was a consequence of human activity."[16]

When the spore findings were published, ecologists and other conservation experts noted that the findings should serve as a reminder for how closely captive-breeding programs ought to monitor their populations. ("Captive breeding is not always a safe haven," *Science* quoted conservation biologist Stuart Pimm when the results of the snail spore-findings were published.[17]) They also noted that the spores were a reminder of just how fragile a species was in the wild to be in a captive breeding program to begin with.

When Turgi died, his story made the media rounds. The *Evening Standard* in London reported that Turgi had been discovered "mo-

15. Ferber, "Bug Vanquishes Species."

16. Andrew A. Cunningham and Peter Daszak, "Extinction of a Species of Land Snail Due to Infection with a Microsporidian Parasite," 1140.

17. Dan Ferber, "Bug Vanquishes Species," 215–16.

tionless in its Perspex box." Newspapers like *Los Angeles Times* wrote that Turgi "moved at a rate of less than 2 feet a year so it took a while for the curators at London Zoo to be sure it had stopped moving forever."[18] (In the *Evening Standard*'s 1996 eulogy, Paul Pearce-Kelly was quick to point out that, of course, the zoo knew Turgi had died. "They are not so slow that you cannot tell they are dead."[19]) Most reported that the species had been put at risk due to the ill-conceived introduction of not one, but two, invasive snail species.

As an endling, Turgi wasn't, perhaps, as grandiose as many of his fellow lasts of their species. He wasn't as furry and charismatic as Benjamin the thylacine, whose death made him a mascot for National Threatened Species Day in Australia. Turgi wasn't a martyr that tourists visit on eco-pilgrimages, like Sudan the northern white rhino almost-endling. He wasn't a stately Lonesome George living out his life with gravitas in his own Galápagos islands. Although sad, of course, reports of Turgi's death were certainly less intentionally pathos-filled than many other eulogies of species' extinctions; perhaps because it's harder to anthropomorphize a snail than other charismatic organisms.

But *Partula* doesn't end with Turgi. Although Turgi's species remains extinct, of course, the story of his sister taxa—other *Partula* species that were part of international breeding programs in Europe and North America—has a different, more hopeful ending. The rosy wolf snail's population has declined on the islands, and captive breeding programs (including the one that Turgi was part of) have continued their work that began in the mid-1980s. In addition to monitoring the decline of the rosy wolf snail, the programs established predator-free enclosures and safe areas for the preyed-upon *Partula*.

18. "Tiny Tree Snail Finally Creeps to Extinction"; "World's Last Polynesian Tree Snail Dies at London Zoo," *The Los Angeles Times,* February 5, 1996, B12.

19. "1,500,000-Year Slow Road to Eternity Is Over for a Tiny Snail."

By 2014, the programs had established robust enough numbers of other *Partula* species that snails could be repatriated to Polynesia by the thousands to reestablish populations in the wild. "To see these animals released into their historic homeland was a very emotional moment," Gerardo Garcia, a curator at Chester Zoo and part of the *Partula* captive breeding project, noted in *The Guardian* in 2019. "Our planet's biodiversity is under threat, every single one of those tiny animals now represents a special symbol of hope."[20]

As of September 2019, more than 15,000 *Partula* snails (from fourteen species and subspecies) have been released on the islands of Huahine and Moorea, between Bora Bora and Tahiti. "*Partula rosea* and *varia* also have a very strong cultural affinity with the people of Huahine, who traditionally used the shells for making crowns and necklaces for special occasions," the Zoological Society of London reported in 2019 when the two *Partula* species that had been extinct in the wild were reintroduced. "Returning the snails to the island is therefore as much a cultural as a conservation celebration."[21]

How we think about and use the concept of "charisma" today is a rather recent, twentieth-century phenomena—one that conservation biology has borrowed from political philosophy and sociology. Charisma's etymological and social history, however, plays a role in the stories, personalities, and even the anthropomorphisms we assign to endangered species, as well as the narratives we draw from to talk about their extinctions and endlings.

20. McKie, "Precious Escargot."

21. "Two Extinct-in-the-Wild Partula Snail Species Returned to the Wild for First Time in 25 Years," Zoological Society of London (ZSL), accessed September 14, 2021, https://www.zsl.org/conservation/news /two-extinct-in-the-wild-partula-snail-species-returned-to-the-wild-for -first-time; "Partula Snail Conservation Programme," Zoological Society of London (ZSL), accessed August 18, 2021, https://www.zsl.org/conservation /regions/oceania/partula-snail-conservation-programme.

The *Oxford English Dictionary* points out that very early uses of "charisma" come from the Greek "*χάρισμα*," although "charisma" does not typically appear in classical Greek or early Christian literature.[22] In the context of the New Testament, it refers to "favour given, gift of grace"; it is alternatively defined as "a divinely conferred power or talent."[23] Seventeenth-century English cleric and prelate Richard Montagu referred to the "The Charismata of grace" in his *Acts & Monuments,* published in 1642; other writers and philosophers prior to the twentieth century kept "charisma" tied to Christian theology and religious institutions.[24]

The idea that charisma is a "gift and power of leadership and authority"[25] comes from the work of German sociologist Max Weber's 1922 publication *Wirtschaft u. Gesellschaft (The Theory of Social and Economic Organization)*; in what the *Oxford English Dictionary* calls a "re-borrowing" of the Greek word rather than an evolution of *charisma*'s original meaning. According to Weber, charisma is "a certain quality of an individual personality, by virtue of which he is set apart from ordinary men and treated as endowed with supernatural, superhuman, or at least specifically exceptional powers or qualities."[26] This definition is still in use in social sciences.

Although Weber's work draws quite a bit from the word's theological history, he saw charisma acting in two ways through modern, not-necessarily-religious political and social institutions, particularly in regard to the question of leadership, authority, and personality—and not always for the better. The first was that charisma could be "a gift that inheres in an object or person simply by virtue of natural endowment." (This is where Weber saw instances of charisma being an inherent trait that could not be acquired.)

22. San Juan, "Orientations of Max Weber's Concept of Charisma," 270.

23. Courchamp et al., "The Paradoxical Extinction of the Most Charismatic Animals," 1.

24. "Charism | Charisma, n.," *OED Online,* accessed September 14, 2021, http://www.oed.com/view/Entry/30721.

25. "Charism | Charisma, n."

26. Weber, *The Theory of Social and Economic Organization,* 359.

The second was that charisma could be "produced artificially in an object or person through some extraordinary means." In other words, charisma could be innate, or it could be learned, or it could be assigned.[27] Charisma is flexible, but it, inevitably, would have a way to connect charismatic people to audiences.

For conservation biology, "charisma," as applied to species with popular appeal, began to appear in scientific literature and conservation efforts, especially fundraising, in the mid- to late-twentieth century.[28] Here is where species (in particular animal species) could be "charismatic" in appeal outside of traditional folk or fairy tales; and charisma—either innate or assigned—could shape their conservation status going forward. It's worth noting that there is a well-documented and long-running concern in conservation biology that the use of "charisma" and "charismatic species" does more harm than good for conservation efforts. Biologists like Frédéric Ducarme, Gloria Luque, and Franck Courchamp, for example, point out that many that oppose—critique, really—the application of charisma in biology do so because of "its deceitfulness for the public, its unscientific character, a wider doubt about surrogate strategies efficiency, and a more particular doubt about the relevance of charismatic species as umbrella or keystone species."[29]

What does this mean for endlings? It certainly means that it's easier to tell endling stories about species that we think of as innately charismatic. (What conservation biologists might call the bias toward large, furry vertebrates.) But, going back to Weber's work with the concept, it's possible to assign charisma to an individual through "extraordinary means"—perhaps this is what other, overlooked endlings and their stories need.

27. San Juan, "Orientations of Max Weber's Concept of Charisma," 272.
28. Jepson and Barua, "A Theory of Flagship Species Action."
29. Courchamp et al., "The Paradoxical Extinction of the Most Charismatic Animals," 4.

It's known in botanical circles as the "loneliest plant." Only one of its kind has even been found in the wild.

This single, solitary tree—a cycad, to be specific—was discovered in what is now KwaZulu-Natal, South Africa, in 1895 by botanist John Medley Wood. The tree—a clump, really, because the tree had several giant trunks and small offsets growing from it—was tucked away on a steep, south-facing slope at the edge of a small granite outcrop in the oNgoye Forest. Wood was the curator of the Durban Botanic Gardens and immediately recognized the cycad's significance as a new, undescribed cycad species.

Cycads are some of the oldest trees on the planet, evolving some 280 million years ago. These Permian plants grew across the earth's supercontinent, Pangea; fossils have been found in North and South America, Europe, Australia, and even Antarctica. Specific cycad species have come and gone, but cycads have been part of earth's natural history for eons. Scientists estimate that during the Jurassic period, cycads made up about 20 percent of the world's plants, leading some paleontologists to refer to the middle Jurassic as the "Age of Cycads."[30]

Cycads are often confused with palm trees, as both plants have scaly trunks and topknots of fronds, but they are not closely related at all. Palm trees are angiosperms—plants that flower and with seeds protected by fruit. Cycads, on the other hand, are gymnosperms—plants whose seeds are exposed in open structures, like conifers that produce a pinecone. Cycads are what botanists call "dioecious," meaning that different male and female parts are not contained in one cycad plant. In other words, there are male and female cycads, and the species needs both to survive.

It's hard to see these plants as anything other than evolutionary survivors. It seems that cycads have an adaption for everything. Cycads' inner seed kernels, for example, are impervious to an elephant's digestive system. Some seeds can float, perhaps even the

30. Jones, *Cycads of the World.*

distance of an ocean. Growing shoots from a parent plant are protected by fire-resistant leaves. Sometimes the plants can change
sex from male to female and vice versa. And they speciate—cycads
are constantly producing new subspecies and hybrids.[31] Over the
course of their evolutionary history, cycads have lived through the
Cretaceous catastrophe that wiped out the dinosaurs, multiple ice
ages, as well as the constant speciation of other plants. (These spe-
ciations included newer and bigger trees, as well as fruiting and
flowering plants.) All of these factors—over hundreds of millions
of years—have pushed cycads into smaller and smaller ecological
niches.

Today, there are fewer and fewer cycads—just over three hundred
extant species—found in the world, where they tend to cluster in
tropical and subtropical climes. Many cycad species are in decline,
and several are on the brink of extinction. (In South Africa, for example, several cycad species have fewer than a hundred individual
plants.[32])

Which brings us back to 1895 and the cycad discovered by John
Medley Wood. The oNgoye forest is now part of an almost four-
thousand-hectare reserve in KwaZulu-Natal, which contains several types of ecotones, depending on altitude, aspect, and soil type.
This particular cycad is tall with an intricate pattern on its trunk
and bright green fronds; its cones are bright orange in color and
each cone can be over a meter in length. In 1903, Wood sent his
assistant, James Wylie, to collect some of the smaller offsets from
the cycad tree—clump—to be cultivated at the Durban Botanic
Gardens. (Wood was a self-trained botanist who was curator of
the Durban Botanic Gardens from 1882 until 1913; he also founded

31. Mabye, *The Cabaret of Plants.*
32. Boglárka Erdei et al., "First Cycad Seedling Foliage from the
Fossil Record and Inferences for the Cenozoic Evolution of Cycads,"
20190114; Jones, *Cycads of the World*; "Meet Durban's Famous Cycad
Family," *South Coast Herald* (blog), accessed September 14, 2021, https://
southcoastherald.co.za/297604/meet-durbans-famous-cycad-family/.

the Natal Herbarium in 1882.) This new cycad species was named *Encephalartos woodii*—commonly called Wood's cycad—in his honor.[33]

Despite a century of looking, no other *E. woodii* individual—more to the point, no female individual—has been found. The cycad plant Wood discovered is it—the first, last, and only individual of *E. woodii* to be found in the wild. (Incidentally, "It is not known what drove Wood's cycad to extinction in the wild, or indeed if it ever was abundant," a Kew Gardens description reads.[34]) At this point, the species cannot naturally reproduce as it has for hundreds of millions of years. And yet, there are hundreds of *E. woodii* plants on earth today.

What kind of endling is this???

Unlike rhinos, ibexes, or even snails, *Encephalartos woodii*—and all cycads—challenges the idea of "an individual." It's easy—straightforward—to see how Celia was an endling and her clone was "her" again; when Celia's clone died, that was that. But cycad plants propagate clones of themselves when they grow offsets and suckers. These clones are genetically identical to their parent plant and can grow to be a new, individual plant, albeit one that is a clone. (For cycads, this is an adaptive strategy if pollination fails.) Thus, there can be several plants that are all clones; because no new traits can evolve in a species that is many clones of a single individual, the species—Wood's cycad—is effectively in an evolutionary holding

33. Robert Krulwich, "The Loneliest Plant In The World," *NPR,* May 10, 2011, https://www.npr.org/sections/krulwich/2011/05/10/136029423 /the-loneliest-plant-in-the-world; Robert Krulwich, "Does the Loneliest Plant in the World Need Help?," *National Geographic,* February 1, 2016, https://www.nationalgeographic.com/science/article/does-the-loneliest -plant-in-the-world-need-help.

34. "Meet the Plant Undateables | Kew," accessed August 24, 2021, https://www.kew.org/read-and-watch/plant-undateables-loneliest-plants -in-world; "Encephalartos Woodii Sander," *Plants of the World Online,* accessed September 14, 2021, http://powo.science.kew.org/taxon/urn:lsid: ipni.org:names:297146-1.

pattern, at the whim of humans to continue to propagate and grow the offsets into adult plants.

When Wylie brought back offsets to the Durban Botanical Gardens, the specimens he collected were male—the same male, technically, as the cycad male parent plant from the oNgoye forest. More offsets from this same, original tree were collected until 1916, when the South African Forestry Department collected the last remaining trunk from the clump, sending it to Pretoria, thus making *Encephalartos woodii* extinct in the wild.[35] (There is some dispute in Wood cycad literature about whether there were two or four trunks of the original plant.[36]) The offsets that Wood and Wylie cultivated remain in the Durban Botanical Gardens to this day; one Durban cycad currently measures upward of two meters (6.5 feet) around the trunk in circumference and weighs more than 2.5 tons.[37]

Wood sent other offsets to other botanical gardens—like Kew Gardens in London, where the plant stayed in the Palm House for the duration of the twentieth century until its move to the Temperate House.[38] ("It's so lonesome and rare that only one specimen has ever been found in the wild," the Kew Gardens website describes.[39]) In addition to the plants at Kew Gardens and Durban Botanical Gardens, Wood's offsets cycads can be found in Longwood Gardens in Pennsylvania, Hortus Botanicus in the Netherlands, and Kirstenbosch National Botanical Garden in Cape Town, to name a few places.

So what does all of this mean for Wood's cycad? Evolutionarily, not much. Since there isn't a—known—female individual, the plant continues to live through propagation. (Cycads live an incredibly

35. "Encephalartos Woodii Sander," *Plants of the World Online.*

36. "Encephalartos Woodii | PlantZAfrica," accessed September 14, 2021, http://pza.sanbi.org/encephalartos-woodii.

37. "Encephalartos Woodii | PlantZAfrica."

38. "Wood Like to Meet: The Loneliest Plant in the World | Kew," accessed September 14, 2021, https://www.kew.org/read-and-watch/wood -like-to-meet-the-loneliest-plant.

39. "Meet the Plant Undateables | Kew."

long time; in some species, an individual plant can live to be a thousand years old.) The new plants from offsets grow the species in number. Botanists have bred a Wood's cycad with a female *E. natalensis* (a closely related cycad species) in the hope of producing hybrids that they can mate and remate with the original offset, over several plant generations, with a genetically intentional female *E. woodii*—or something close enough. There is also the small, small hope that one of the plants might spontaneously change sex, thus providing the species with a natural female plant.

Years ago, I visited Kirstenbosch Botanical Gardens in Cape Town and walked through the garden's cycad amphitheater of "living fossils," where the gardens grow close to forty different cycad species that are endemic to South Africa, including the plant that was sent by James Wood in 1916 from the Durban Botanical Gardens. ("At Kirstenbosch the base of the trunk is obscured by a cage that surrounds [the] plant, put there in the 1980s to prevent suckers from being stolen again," the website for the South African national Biodiversity Institute informs us.[40]) When I visited, I understood that many of the cycad species were endangered, but I hadn't quite grasped that one of them—*E. woodii*—was a plant that had been cultivated as an offset from the Wood's cycad endling. It's a chastening, humbling feeling to realize you hiked by an endling and—due to your own ignorance—didn't know it.

The Wood's cycad endling is, literally, legion. It's one individual, but it is in many places, and each of those places can propagate their own offsets—their own clones—with so much less techno-wizardry and intensive laboratory work than went into Celia's seven minutes of de-extinction. There are Wood's cycads around the world in various collections, prized by many private collectors much in the same way they would a painting or rare curio.

Consequently, this is a very different sort of endling story than that of Benjamin, Celia, or even the little snail Turgi—a cycad is not

40. "Encephalartos Woodii | PlantZAfrica."

easily anthropomorphized, and even if it were, it doesn't quite fit how we've come to think about other endling stories. Rather than a story that uses a particularly charismatic actor or character, "plants can offer a way to tell stories about collectives, rather than individuals," literary scholar and former biologist Devin Griffiths explained to me. Griffiths's own research traces how Charles Darwin wrote about plants and plant narratives. "Exploring plants and plant-based narratives are a way to break down a plant–human divide."[41]

Because of its biology and evolutionary history, its endling narrative will be different. It's not a Last Survivor—not exactly—and it's not a character in an Aesop fable. Wood's cycad doesn't have a nickname or a persona. (Other than being a "lonely" plant.) The pathos that comes with the death of an individual and a species so very near extinction is mitigated a bit because, well, there are other clones of the last plant. The species, however, is now dependent on human care and cultivation for its survival.

Incas the Carolina parakeet, Turgi the tree snail, Wood's cycad, and myriad other endlings remind us that charisma is, for better or worse, an integral part of how we talk about extinction and how we frame extinction stories.

These endlings, and their stories, might not get as much press coverage and attention as Sudan, Fatu, and Najin—the northern white rhinos—but these other, perhaps less charismatic endlings, are hardly alone in their existence. (The Kew Gardens website, for example, points out that they have other "lonely" and "last" plants in their collections beyond Wood's cycad; plants like *Hyophorbe amaricaulis,* a palm tree endemic to the island of Mauritius; *Cypripedium calceolus,* the British lady's slipper orchid; and *Ramosmania rodriguesii*, commonly known as café marron, from the island of Rodrigues in the Indian Ocean. In the instances of the orchid and

<hr>

41. Devin Griffiths, Zoom interview with author, September 9, 2021; Griffiths, "Great Exaptations."

café marron, the gardens were able to repropagate the plant out of its endling status, although these they are still considered extinct in the wild.[42]) But they are still endling stories, regardless of whether we consider the endlings charismatic or not; they still show how we humans mark the extinction—or almost extinction—of a species.

Perhaps endlings could be a way of telling stories about species that we don't typically see as charismatic (invertebrates, plants, the like), functioning as a set of flagship stories for the narratives of species extinctions. After all, we have decided how to imbue and read species' charisma in the past; what's to prevent charisma from evolving to encompass other endling stories?

Perhaps charisma's flexibility could be its greatest storytelling asset.

42. "Meet the Plant Undateables | Kew."

Conclusion: How Do You Say "Endling" In isiZulu?

TO DATE, the word *endling* only appears in English.

"When I come across 'endling' in Spanish, Catalan, or Aragonese literature, it's the English word simply situated in a non-English language," geographer Adam Searle told me. "When referencing Celia or Laña, we usually see '*última*' used instead of 'endling.'" (*Última* is "last," "final," or—if you prefer a cognate—"ultimate.") Searle paused. "But '*última*' doesn't quite carry the same connotation as 'endling.'"[1]

Other English words that are extinction-adjacent to *endling* (like *Anthropocene*) have made their way into non-English languages. "In Swedish, we use *Antropocen* to talk about the Anthropocene era," environmental historian Dolly Jørgensen offered. "It's borrowed directly from English. But there isn't a word for 'endling' in Swedish or Norwegian that I know of."[2]

If the word *endling* is only an English one—and, remember, it's a recent word at that—it might help unpack why endling stories seem to be so heavily influenced by an English- and a Western-based literary canon. (Although it's worth keeping in mind that many folktales and fairy tales carry with them an arguably "universal

1. Searle, interview.
2. Jørgensen, interview.

element" to their narratives[3]), In other words, why it's so easy for endling stories to be framed through epic poems like *Beowulf.*

But new words evolve all the time—on average, for example, English adds something like a thousand new words a year to its colloquial lexicon—and in a raft of different contexts.[4] The constant evolution of language and the adaptability of its structural narratives is part of how such stories have endured for millennia.

What if *endling* made a linguistic leap outside of English? What would that leap mean for the word, how we think about endlings, and the sorts of stories we tell about them?

There are three ways that *endling* could enter non-English storytelling. (This is nothing new; words and stories cross languages and cultures all the time.) If—when, rather—the word radiates from its English root, there is a potential for a multitude of storytelling and new narratives. The word gives space for character and narrative development.

First, *endling* could function as a "loanword" or "foreign word" the way words like *café* or *bazaar* or *pasta* are integrated into languages that aren't their original French, Persian, or Italian. This approach would mean that *endling* is simply adopted from English and slotted into a non-English language. (*"Celia fue la última bucardo; ella es una endling."* "Celia was the last bucardo; she is an endling." Incidentally, in this instance, Google Translate offers "final" for "endling.") Second, *endling* could be transformed, keeping its English base but adapting into non-English languages in flexible ways. In languages like isiZulu, for example, the prefix "i-" has become a way to deal with hard-to-translate terms; *endling* could

3. Barthes and Duisit, "An Introduction to the Structural Analysis of Narrative"; Nakawake and Sato, "Systematic Quantitative Analyses Reveal the Folk-Zoological Knowledge Embedded in Folktales."

4. Andy Bodle, "How New Words Are Born," *The Guardian,* February 4, 2016, https://www.theguardian.com/media/mind-your-language/2016/feb/04/english-neologisms-new-words.

be translated as *i-endling*. This allows languages a flexibility to incorporate new words and to then remake them into their own. (This sort of word borrowing is not a favored translation practice in isiZulu, however.) Keeping the word situated in English, for better or worse, centers the concept and endling stories in a traditionally Western canon of storytelling.

The third option is the most intriguing one. What if new words for endlings were created? The English word was invented out of need. It's hard to imagine that, over a quarter of a century and hundreds and hundreds of species extinctions later, this need is any less or that the need is strictly confined to English. Could other "endling" words transform how people think about and talk about species that are going extinct in their own lifetimes?

In short, yes. Yes, it could. And recent work with isiZulu and decolonizing science writing shows what that might look like.

"There's no word for *dinosaur* in isiZulu." Nor are there words for *Jurassic, fossilization,* or *evolution,* South African science journalist and isiZulu-speaker Sibusiso Biyela explained to me as we talked about species, fossils, and endlings, reiterating what he had written in 2019 on the topic for *The Open Notebook,* a nonprofit science journalism organization.[5] Biyela is part of a large research project team called Decolonise Science that plans to translate 180 scientific papers published in English into six African languages—isiZulu and Northern Sotho from southern Africa; Hausa and Yoruba from West Africa; and Luganda and Amharic from East Africa.[6]

In 2019, Biyela published a poignant essay in *The Open Notebook* about translating an English story of a new dinosaur species discovery in South Africa into isiZulu for isiZulu readers. In the piece, he described how he augmented words and phrases in isiZulu to explain the object or concept. "I translated *fossil* as *Amathambo*

5. Sibusiso Biyela, "Decolonizing Science Writing in South Africa," *The Open Notebook,* February 12, 2019, https://www.theopennotebook.com /2019/02/12/decolonizing-science-writing-in-south-africa/.

6. Wild, "African Languages to Get More Bespoke Scientific Terms."

amadala atholakala emhlabathini," he offered by way of example, using an example from his *Open Notebook* publication, "old bones found in the ground."[7]

I was curious how this sort of storytelling via translation would carry over into endlings. "There currently isn't a word for endling in isiZulu," Biyela confirmed.[8] But this doesn't mean that there couldn't be one.

"There are campaigns all the time to save the rhino. But they've never been done in isiZulu, which is disappointing," Biyela noted.[9] "I've seen officials who have tried all sorts of approaches to try to stop poaching, to connect with the communities in the areas where poaching happens. But I've never seen them use local languages to do so." As the third most biodiverse country in the world, South Africa does have a long history of wildlife management and conservation throughout the twentieth- and twenty-first centuries, with various approaches mapping onto different periods of the country's politics.[10] Moreover, South Africa has eleven official languages. Historically, wildlife conservation campaigns have been carried out primarily in English and Afrikaans—languages that carry with them a problematic colonial legacy, to put it mildly. (And, of course, scientific publications are primarily in English.) Even a cursory internet search about specific wildlife campaigns shows the majority of information to appear only in English, without the website itself offering non-English translation options outside of Google Translate.

"In my research, I see language evolving with wildlife," South African PhD student and isiZulu-speaker Fortunate Mafeta Phaka explained to me. His work focuses on biocultural diversity of her-

7. Biyela, "Decolonizing Science Writing in South Africa"; Sibusiso Biyela, Zoom interview with author, May 18, 2021.

8. Biyela, interview.

9. Biyela, interview.

10. Carruthers, "Conservation and Wildlife Management in South African National Parks 1930s–1960s"; Gissibl, "Colony or Zoological Garden?"

petofauna in South Africa. A founder of Wildlife in Vernacular, he is also the author of *A Bilingual Guide to the Frogs of Zululand*. "If you look at the extinction of biodiversity, it coincides with extinction of language diversity. It would make sense that language will evolve with wildlife."[11] Words, ideas, and story structure change, adapt, and evolve between languages. "Maybe if there was some sort of campaign that uses words like *endling*, it would have more impact," Biyela suggested. "*Endling* carries a punch. We don't have the word, but we need it."

What would that word be? I asked. Biyela looked thoughtful. He started typing into the Zoom chat window and said, "There. *Isilwane sokugcina kuhlobo*. This is how I think *endling* would be in isiZulu."[12]

He talked me through his translation, "'*Isigcino*'—the root being '*-gcino*'—means 'final' or 'end,'" Biyela explained. "In the context of the word *endling* being used in a sentence without modification, then '*isigcino*' can be used in equivalence but if a person were to specify that a certain animal is 'last of its species' then I would say that it is '*isilwane sokugcina kuhlobo*,' where '*isilwane*' is *animal* and '*-uhlobo*' is 'species.'"[13]

And just like that, a new word was born. And with it, I'm sure, new storytelling possibilities.

"The word has been out for decades: We were born on a damaged planet careening toward environmental collapse," anthropologist Vincent Ialenti points out. "Yet our intellects are poorly equipped to grasp the scale of the Earth's ecological death spiral."[14]

Philosophers, historians, activists, and conservations have long grappled with these "what if" questions in terms of extinction,

11. Fortunate Mafeta Phaka, Zoom interview with author, June 2, 2021.

12. Biyela, interview.

13. Sibusiso Biyela, interview with author, September 2, 2021; Biyela, interview with author, May 18, 2021.

14. Ialenti, "The Art of Pondering Distant Future Earths."

broadly, and endlings, specifically. "In each instance, extinction seems to require us to ask what will this loss mean and for whom?" philosopher Thom Van Dooren writes. "What would be the costs of stemming it, and again, for whom? And so, ultimately, extinction asks us to consider what kind of relationships we want to cultivate in this place at this time."[15]

Grief and mourning are common elements that run through how we tell stories of endlings, framed, in no small part, by a pressing need to make sense of the scale of species death that people living in the sixth mass extinction will, and have, witnessed. How we mourn, how we come to grips with watching the last known individual of a species die, requires language and a narrative framing that acknowledges its gravity. The sorts of stories and narratives that we've used to talk about endlings—folktales, fairy tales, and the like—are no strangers to being read as narratives of trauma and grief.

There's a lot of despair in the world right now. I wrote *Endlings* during a global pandemic, as countries locked down over and over to try and stop the spread of the disease, watching global deaths from Covid-19 counted in the millions. Wildfires burn across the world. Glaciers melt. Social inequality is rampant; immigration policies draconian. As I typed up some of the project's interview notes, the Intergovernmental Panel on Climate Change issued its 2021 report that basically said, "We're screwed."

I spent a not insignificant amount of writing time wondering: What if? What if humankind had made better decisions in the centuries ramping up to our point here today? Decisions that didn't leave us with over one million species currently threatened with extinction?[16] That didn't result in 150 new endlings dying every

15. Van Dooren, "Extinction," 178.

16. Martin, "UN Report: Nature's Dangerous Decline 'Unprecedented'; Species Extinction Rates 'Accelerating,'" *United Nations Sustainable Development* (blog), accessed August 10, 2021, https://www.un.org /sustainabledevelopment/blog/2019/05/nature-decline-unprecedented -report.

day? What if—in the unraveling exosystemic relationships, the breakdown of generations of lifeways, the new ways of grieving that extinction prompts—we had simply picked something else?[17] What if—for all of the Benjamins, the Lonesome Georges, the Celias, the Turgis, the Qi Qis—whatever action we muster up isn't enough?

And yet. The thread of hope, I found, came from *isilwane sokugcina kuhlobo*. It was like watching the inverse of extinction; it was watching language and storytelling speciate.

We are living in an Age of Endlings, but we might also be living at a point were endling storytelling (in English and non-English) could shape the way we think about extinction and the animal stories we curate and share. Perhaps recognizing and improving endling storytelling—maybe, just maybe— could offer something other than despair.

We owe it to these endlings to tell their stories in as many words and narratives as possible.

17. Van Dooren, "Extinction," 172–73.

Acknowledgments

I am very grateful to the many, many people who have contributed their time, expertise, enthusiasm, and scholarship to helping me with this project. *Endlings* would have been impossible without them.

Specifically, I would like to thank: Elaine Ayers, Ross Barnett, Sibusiso Biyela, Laura Briscoe, Claire Cameron, Mackenzie Cooley, Devin Griffiths, Eddie Guimont, Dolly Jørgensen, Marc Kissel, Siu Kwan Lam, Alison Laurence, John Leavitt, Adrianna Link, Ilja Nieuwland, Eleanor Parker, David Petts, Fortunate Mafeta Phaka, Nick Pyenson, Megan Raby, Julien Riel-Salvatore, Lukas Rieppel, Douglass Rovinsky, Gessica Sakamoto Martini, Christopher Schaberg, Adam Searle, Kate Sheppard, Anna Toledano, Sarah Wild, and Kate Wiles. The "Writing Accountability Group" that Elaine Ayers facilitated in 2021 offered its unending enthusiasm and support for this project with many, many brilliant suggestions from friends and colleagues for ways to think about the materials.

The research for this project was made possible through my affiliate appointment with the University of Texas at Austin's Institute for Historical Studies and the library and resource access that brings; Courtney Meador's tireless administrative efforts ensure that my appointment shows up every academic year. I would also like to acknowledge Steven P. as well as the students, faculty, and volunteers in the Pen-City Writers Program; they have all encouraged and challenged me to think about writing in new, complex ways.

I am grateful to my editors, Doug Armato and Eric Lundgren, at University of Minnesota Press, for their interest in including *Endlings* in the press's Forerunners series and for their thoughts, recommendations, and patience in bringing *Endlings* from "idea" to "book." I would also like to thank Mike Stoffel for copyediting and Anne Carter for production and editorial assistance. Holly Zemsta's edits and suggestions were much appreciated in the project's early drafts as was Rachel Garner's fact-checking of a near-complete draft.

As always, I appreciate my parents' support of the book writing process and their interest in the topic. I am most grateful to my husband, Stan, for his never-failing belief and optimism in this—and every—book project. And our daughter, Esther, was kind enough to share her illustrated copy of *Aesop's Fables* with me while *Endlings* was being written.

Further Reading

A book like *Endlings* is only possible thanks to decades of scholarship conducted by people in a plethora of disciplines. I am immensely grateful that so many scholars and storytellers have so generously shared their work, their time, and their expertise with me for *Endlings*.

I found myself interested in exploring endlings as a topic after reading Maria Dahvana Headley's 2020 translation of *Beowulf*. I came across her use of the word *extinct* in the text to be fantastically striking and offered—to my thinking—a connection between a very old piece of literature and the nature of living in an Age of Endlings in the Anthropocene today. Her translation made me wonder what other characters and stories could shape and be shaped by the those that are "the last of their kind."

This project hopes to build on such brilliant, painstaking work—to bring together examples and ideas from different disciplines to highlight ways that we could talk about endlings and storytelling. The references that I've included in the project's bibliography are in no way meant to be considered a comprehensive literature review on any of the topics in this book; they are simply the sources that I drew from most directly from for the project's text.

For readers who are interested in a deeper dive into these topics, I would recommend the following:

Fuller, Errol. *Lost Animals: Extinction and the Photographic Record.* Princeton, N.J.: Princeton University Press, 2013.

Heise, Ursula K. *Imagining Extinction: The Cultural Meanings of Endangered Species.* Chicago: University of Chicago Press, 2016.

Hennessy, Elizabeth. *On the Backs of Tortoises: Darwin, the Galápagos, and the Fate of an Evolutionary Eden.* New Haven, Conn.: Yale University Press, 2019.

Jørgensen, Dolly. *Recovering Lost Species in the Modern Age: Histories of Longing and Belonging.* Cambridge, Mass.: MIT Press, 2019.

Paddle, Robert. *The Last Tasmanian Tiger: The History and Extinction of the Thylacine.* Cambridge: Cambridge University Press, 2000.

Turvey, Samuel. *Witness to Extinction: How We Failed to Save the Yangtze River Dolphin.* Oxford: Oxford University Press, 2008.

Van Dooren, Thom. *Flight Ways: Life and Loss at the Edge of Extinction.* New York: Columbia University Press, 2014.

Bibliography

Barthes, Roland, and Lionel Duisit. "An Introduction to the Structural Analysis of Narrative." *New Literary History* 6, no. 2 (1975): 237–72. https://doi.org/10.2307/468419.

Bettelheim, Bruno. *The Uses of Enchantment: The Meaning and Importance of Fairy Tales*. New York: Vintage, 2010.

Bicho, Nuno, Antonio F. Carvalho, Cesar González-Sainz, Jose Luis Sanchidrián, Valentín Villaverde, and Lawrence G. Straus. "The Upper Paleolithic Rock Art of Iberia." *Journal of Archaeological Method and Theory* 14, no. 1 (March 1, 2007): 81–151. https://doi.org/10.1007/s10816 -007-9025-5.

Biyela, Sibusiso. "Decolonizing Science Writing in South Africa." *The Open Notebook*, February 12, 2019. https://www.theopennotebook.com/2019 /02/12/decolonizing-science-writing-in-south-africa/.

Bressan, David. "Thomas Jefferson's Patriotic Monsters." *Scientific American Blog Network*. Accessed February 27, 2022. https://blogs .scientificamerican.com/history-of-geology/thomas-jefferson-8217-s -patriotic-monsters/.

Carruthers, Jane. "Conservation and Wildlife Management in South African National Parks 1930s–1960s." *Journal of the History of Biology* 41, no. 2 (2008): 203–36.

Church, George M., and Edward Regis. *Regenesis: How Synthetic Biology Will Reinvent Nature and Ourselves*. New York: Basic Books, 2014.

Clayton, Edward. "Aesop, Aristotle, and Animals: The Role of Fables in Human Life." *Humanitas* 21, no. 1–2 (2008): 179–200.

Cokinos, Christopher. "The Carolina Parakeet Reminds Us to Do Better." *Pacific Standard*. Accessed September 14, 2021. https://psmag.com /environment/remembering-the-carolina-parakeet.

Courchamp, Franck, Ivan Jaric, Céline Albert, Yves Meinard, William J. Ripple, and Guillaume Chapron. "The Paradoxical Extinction of the Most Charismatic Animals." *PLoS Biology* 16, no. 4 (April 12, 2018): e2003997. https://doi.org/10.1371/journal.pbio.2003997.

Crane, Brent. "Chasing the World's Most Endangered Turtle." *The New Yorker.* Accessed September 14, 2021. https://www.newyorker.com /science/elements/chasing-the-worlds-rarest-turtle.

Cunningham, Andrew A., and Peter Daszak. "Extinction of a Species of Land Snail Due to Infection with a Microsporidian Parasite." *Conservation Biology* 12, no. 5 (1998): 1139–41.

Cunningham, Andrew A., Peter Daszak, Shaheed K. Macgregor, Ian Foster, David Clarke, and Paul Pearce-Kelly. "Mortality of Endangered Snails of the Genus *Partula*: Preliminary Results of Pathologic Investigations." *Journal of Zoo and Wildlife Medicine* 27, no. 1 (1996): 19–27.

Dooren, Thom van. *Flight Ways: Life and Loss at the Edge of Extinction.* New York: Columbia University Press, 2014.

Ducarme, Frédéric, Gloria M. Luque, and Franck Courchamp. "What Are 'Charismatic Species' for Conservation Biologists?" *BioSciences Master Reviews,* July 2013, 8.

Erdei, Boglárka, Mario Coiro, Ian Miller, Kirk R. Johnson, M. Patrick Griffith, and Vickie Murphy. "First Cycad Seedling Foliage from the Fossil Record and Inferences for the Cenozoic Evolution of Cycads." *Biology Letters* 15, no. 7 (July 26, 2019): 20190114. https://doi.org/10 .1098/rsbl.2019.0114.

Ferber, Dan. "Bug Vanquishes Species." *Science* 282, no. 5387 (1998): 215.

Fuller, Errol. *Lost Animals: Extinction and the Photographic Record.* Princeton, N.J.: Princeton University Press, 2014.

Gander, Kashmira. "10 Species Still Around That Might Not Be in 2030." *Newsweek,* January 1, 2020. https://www.newsweek.com/10-species -extinct-2030-1479835.

García-González, Ricardo. "New Holocene *Capra Pyrenaica* (Mammalia, Artiodactyla, Bovidae) Skulls from the Southern Pyrénées." *Comptes Rendus Palevol* 11, no. 4 (May 1, 2012): 241–49. https://doi.org/10.1016/j .crpv.2011.12.006.

Giaimo, Cara. "Thomas Jefferson Built This Country on Mastodons." *Atlas Obscura.* http://www.atlasobscura.com/articles/thomas-jefferson -built-this-country-on-mastodons.

Gissibl, Bernhard. "Colony or Zoological Garden? Settlers, Science, and the State." In *The Nature of German Imperialism: Conservation and the Politics of Wildlife in Colonial East Africa,* 141–77. Oxford, UK: Berghahn Books, 2019.

"Global Extinction Rates: Why Do Estimates Vary So Wildly?" *Yale E360.* Accessed September 13, 2021. https://e360.yale.edu/features/global _extinction_rates_why_do_estimates_vary_so_wildly.

González Zarandona, José Antonio. *Murujuga: Rock Art, Heritage, and Landscape Iconoclasm,* Philadelphia: University of Pennsylvania Press, 2020.

Griffiths, Devin. "Great Exaptations: On Reading Darwin's Plant Narratives." In *Narrative in Science: Reasoning, Representing, and Knowing since 1800,* ed. Mary S. Morgan, Kim M. Hajek, and Dominic J. Berry. Cambridge: London School of Economics, 2022.

Hartigan, John, Jr. *Aesop's Anthropology: A Multispecies Approach.* Minneapolis: University of Minnesota Press, 2014.

Headley, Maria Dahvana. *Beowulf: A New Translation.* New York: FSG, 2020.

Heise, Ursula K. *Imagining Extinction: The Cultural Meanings of Endangered Species.* Chicago: University of Chicago Press, 2016.

Hennessy, Elizabeth. *On the Backs of Tortoises: Darwin, the Galapagos, and the Fate of an Evolutionary Eden.* New Haven, Conn.: Yale University Press, 2019.

Ialenti, Vincent. "The Art of Pondering Distant Future Earths." *The MIT Press Reader,* August 10, 2021. https://thereader.mitpress.mit.edu/the -art-of-pondering-distant-future-earths/.

Jepson, Paul, and Maan Barua. "A Theory of Flagship Species Action." *Conservation and Society* 13 (January 1, 2015): 95. https://doi.org/10 .4103/0972-4923.161228.

Jones, David L. *Cycads of the World: Ancient Plants in Today's Landscape,* 2d ed. Washington, D.C.: Smithsonian Books, 2002.

Jørgensen, Dolly. "Endling, the Power of the Last in an Extinction-Prone World." *Environmental Philosophy,* May 17, 2017. https://doi.org/10 .5840/envirophil201612542.

Jørgensen, Dolly. "Presence of Absence, Absence of Presence, and Extinction Narratives." In *Nature, Temporality and Environmental Management: Scandinavian and Australian Perspectives on Peoples and Landscapes,.* ed. Lesley Head, Katarina Saltzman, Gunhild Setten, and Marie Stenseke, 45–58. Abingdon, UK: Routledge, 2016.

Jørgensen, Dolly. *Recovering Lost Species in the Modern Age.* Cambridge, Mass.: MIT Press, 2019.

Kolbert, Elizabeth. "The Lost World." *The New Yorker,* December 8, 2013. http://www.newyorker.com/magazine/2013/12/16/the-lost-world-2.

Kolbert, Elizabeth. *The Sixth Extinction: An Unnatural History.* London: Picador, 2015.

Krulwich, Robert. "Does the Loneliest Plant in the World Need Help?" *National Geographic,* February 1, 2016. https://www .nationalgeographic.com/science/article/does-the-loneliest-plant-in -the-world-need-help.

Lawson, Tom. *The Last Man: A British Genocide in Tasmania.* London: I. B. Tauris, 2014.

Lévi-Strauss, Claude. *Totemism.* Trans. Rodney Needham. Boston: Beacon Press, 1971.

Mabye, Richard. *The Cabaret of Plants: Forty Thousand Years of Plant Life and the Human Imagination.* New York: Norton, 2017.

Monsó, Susana. "Animals Wrestle with the Concept of Death and
    Mortality." *Aeon.* Accessed September 16, 2021. https://aeon.co/essays
    /animals-wrestle-with-the-concept-of-death-and-mortality.
Morton, Timothy. *Realist Magic: Objects, Ontology, Causality.* London:
    Open Humanities Press, 2013.
Nakawake, Yo, and Kosuke Sato. "Systematic Quantitative Analyses
    Reveal the Folk-Zoological Knowledge Embedded in Folktales."
    Palgrave Communications 5, no. 1 (December 17, 2019): 1–10. https://doi
    .org/10.1057/s41599-019-0375-x.
Nicholls, Henry. *Lonesome George: The Life and Loves of a Conservation
    Icon.* London: Palgrave Macmillan, 2006.
Nijhuis, Michelle. "What Do You Call the Last of a Species?" *The New
    Yorker.* Accessed December 22, 2020. https://www.newyorker.com
    /tech/annals-of-technology/what-do-you-call-the-last-of-a-species.
Paddle, Robert. *The Last Tasmanian Tiger: The History and Extinction of
    the Thylacine.* Cambridge: Cambridge University Press, 2002.
Phaka, Fortunate M., Edward C. Netherlands, Donnavan J. D. Kruger,
    and Louis H. Du Preez. "Folk Taxonomy and Indigenous Names
    for Frogs in Zululand, South Africa." *Journal of Ethnobiology and
    Ethnomedicine* 15, no. 1 (March 26, 2019): 17. https://doi.org/10.1186
    /s13002-019-0294-3.
Probyn-Rapsey, Fiona. "Anthropocentrism." In *Critical Terms in Animals
    Studies,* ed. Lori Greun, 47–63. Chicago: University of Chicago Press,
    2018.
Propp, Vladimir Yakovlevich, and Jack Zipes. *The Russian Folktale,* ed.
    Sibelan Forrester. Detroit, Mich.: Wayne State University Press, 2012.
Reynolds, Evelyn. "Beowulf's Poetics of Absorption: Narrative Syntax and
    the Illusion of Stability in the Fight with Grendel's Mother." *Essays in
    Medieval Studies* 31, no. 1 (2015): 43–64. https://doi.org/10.1353/ems
    .2015.0003.
Ross, Nanci J. "'What's That Called?' Folk Taxonomy and Connecting
    Students to the Human–Nature Interface." In *Innovative Strategies for
    Teaching in the Plant Sciences,* ed. Cassandra L. Quave, 121–34. New
    York: Springer, 2014. https://doi.org/10.1007/978-1-4939-0422-8_8.
Saikku, Mikko. "The Extinction of the Carolina Parakeet." *Environmental
    History Review* 14, no. 3 (1990): 1–18. https://doi.org/10.2307/3984724.
San Juan, E. "Orientations of Max Weber's Concept of Charisma." *The
    Centennial Review* 11, no. 2 (1967): 270–85.
Searle, Adam. "Anabiosis and the Liminal Geographies of De/Extinction."
    Environmental Humanities 12, no. 1 (May 1, 2020): 321–45. https://doi
    .org/10.1215/22011919-8142385.
Searle, Adam. "Hunting Ghosts: On Spectacles of Spectrality and the
    Trophy Animal." *Cultural Geographies* 28, no. 3 (January 18, 2021), 513–
    30. https://doi.org/10.1177/1474474020987250.

Searle, Adam. "Spectral Ecologies: De/Extinction in the Pyrenees." *Transactions of the Institute of British Geographers* 47 (2022): 167–83.

Searle, Adam. "A Tale of Two Bucardo: Laña, Celia, and the Contested Meanings of Animal Remains." In *Animal Remains,* ed. Sarah Bezan and Robert McKay, 87–100. London: Routledge, 2022.

Sleightholme, Stephen. "Confirmation of the Gender of the Last Captive Thylacine." *Australian Zoologist* 35 (January 1, 2011): 953–56. https://doi.org/10.7882/AZ.2011.047.

Smith, Daniel, Philip Schlaepfer, Katie Major, Mark Dyble, Abigail E. Page, James Thompson, Nikhil Chaudhary, et al. "Cooperation and the Evolution of Hunter-Gatherer Storytelling." *Nature Communications* 8, no. 1 (December 5, 2017): 1853. https://doi.org/10.1038/s41467-017-02036-8.

TallBear, Kim. "An Indigenous Reflection on Working beyond the Human–Not Human." *GLQ: A Journal of Lesbian and Gay Studies* 21, no. 2/3 (2015): 230–35.

Turvey, Samuel. *Witness to Extinction: How We Failed to Save the Yangtze River Dolphin.* New York: Oxford University Press, 2009.

Van Dooren, Thom. "Extinction." In *Critical Terms in Animal Studies.* Chicago: University of Chicago Press, 2018.

Van Dooren, Thom *Flight Ways: Life and Loss at the Edge of Extinction.* New York: Columbia University Press, 2014.

Weber, Max. *The Theory of Social and Economic Organization.* New York: Henderson and Parson, 1947.

Webster, Robert M., and Bruce Erickson. "The Last Word?" *Nature* 380, no. 6573 (April 1996): 386–86. https://doi.org/10.1038/380386c0.

Wild, Sarah. "African Languages to Get More Bespoke Scientific Terms." *Nature* 596, no. 7873 (August 18, 2021): 469–70. https://doi.org/10.1038/d41586-021-02218-x.

Wilkins, John S. *Defining Species: A Sourcebook from Antiquity to Today.* New York: Peter Lang Publishing, Inc., 2009.

Wilkins, John S. *Species: A History of the Idea.,* Berkeley: University of California Press, 2011.

Wimpenny, Jo. *Aesop's Animals: The Science behind the Fables.* Totnes in Devon, UK: Bloomsbury Sigma, 2021.

Yong, Ed. "The Last of Its Kind." *The Atlantic,* June 25, 2019. https://www.theatlantic.com/magazine/archive/2019/07/extinction-endling-care/590617/.

(Continued from page iii)

Forerunners: Ideas First

Aaron Jaffe
Spoiler Alert: A Critical Guide

Don Ihde
Medical Technics

Jonathan Beecher Field
Town Hall Meetings and the Death of Deliberation

Jennifer Gabrys
How to Do Things with Sensors

Naa Oyo A. Kwate
**Burgers in Blackface: Anti-Black Restaurants
Then and Now**

Arne De Boever
Against Aesthetic Exceptionalism

Steve Mentz
Break Up the Anthropocene

John Protevi
Edges of the State

Matthew J. Wolf-Meyer
**Theory for the World to Come: Speculative Fiction
and Apocalyptic Anthropology**

Nicholas Tampio
Learning versus the Common Core

Kathryn Yusoff
A Billion Black Anthropocenes or None

Kenneth J. Saltman
The Swindle of Innovative Educational Finance

Ginger Nolan
The Neocolonialism of the Global Village

Joanna Zylinska
The End of Man: A Feminist Counterapocalypse

Robert Rosenberger
Callous Objects: Designs against the Homeless

William E. Connolly
**Aspirational Fascism: The Struggle for Multifaceted
Democracy under Trumpism**

Chuck Rybak
UW Struggle: When a State Attacks Its University

Clare Birchall
**Shareveillance: The Dangers of Openly Sharing
and Covertly Collecting Data**

la paperson
A Third University Is Possible

Kelly Oliver
Carceral Humanitarianism: Logics of Refugee Detention

P. David Marshall
The Celebrity Persona Pandemic

Davide Panagia
Ten Theses for an Aesthetics of Politics

David Golumbia
The Politics of Bitcoin: Software as Right-Wing Extremism

Sohail Daulatzai
Fifty Years of *The Battle of Algiers*: Past as Prologue

Gary Hall
The Uberfication of the University

Mark Jarzombek
Digital Stockholm Syndrome in the Post-Ontological Age

N. Adriana Knouf
How Noise Matters to Finance

Andrew Culp
Dark Deleuze

Akira Mizuta Lippit
**Cinema without Reflection: Jacques Derrida's Echopoiesis
and Narcissism Adrift**

Sharon Sliwinski
Mandela's Dark Years: A Political Theory of Dreaming

Grant Farred
Martin Heidegger Saved My Life

Ian Bogost
The Geek's Chihuahua: Living with Apple

Shannon Mattern
Deep Mapping the Media City

Steven Shaviro
No Speed Limit: Three Essays on Accelerationism

Jussi Parikka
The Anthrobscene

Reinhold Martin
Mediators: Aesthetics, Politics, and the City

John Hartigan Jr.
Aesop's Anthropology: A Multispecies Approach

Lydia Pyne is a writer whose most recent books include *Postcards: The Rise and Fall of the World's First Social Network* and *Genuine Fakes: How Phony Things Can Teach Us about Real Stuff.*